Decorating With Color

Decorating With Color

Inspired Ideas for Your Home

BETTERWAY BOOKS

Cincinnati, OH

Visit our Web site at www.artistsnetwork.com for information on more resources for artists.

04 03 02 01 00   5 4 3 2 1

A catalog record for this book is available from the U.S. Library of Congress.

ISBN 1-55870-573-2

Editorial Production Manager: Kathi Howard
Production Coordinator: Sara Dumford
Studio Manager: Ruth Preston

Contents

CHAPTER 1

A Sense of Color

Color KNOW-HOW

The human eye can see over ten million colors, and the shades and tones around us affect how we feel, look and behave. No wonder it is so important to learn how to use color with confidence before decorating your home.

The first thing we notice about a room is the color scheme. It may not be a conscious reaction, but we all respond to the mood created by the colors and patterns used on the walls, ceiling, floor and upholstery in a room. Color in interior design relates to the pigments and dyes that are used to give color to paints, stains and inks. These pigments and dyes start as a pure color or hue, and are lightened or darkened by adding white or black, or are given a subtle midtone by mixing with gray. All these variations spring from the basic pure colors that appear on that useful planning aid—the color wheel.

Variations of one color

A color scheme using different shades of one color is easy on the eye and creates a relaxed atmosphere. In this predominantly green bathroom, the palest tone used for the ceiling and upper walls contrasts comfortably with the darker green paneling below. This type of scheme, known as a monochromatic, or one-color, scheme, needs highlights in a completely different color. In this room these highlights are provided by the dainty mauve wisteria stenciling, the brass faucets and yellow-gold accessories.

With no strong color contrasts to stimulate the eye, rooms decorated in a mixture of colors that lie next to each other on the color wheel (see page 4) are comfortable to live in. This living room uses the orange-to-brown section of the wheel, with colors ranging from pale yellowish tones in the natural wood, through dull orange and terra-cotta to darker brown. Touches of dark blue and light cream and oatmeal colors have been used as accents; without these, the overall effect would be flat and uninteresting.

DULUX

Color contrasts

Schemes with very strong contrasts, such as this mix of yellows with white and black, can be very stimulating—even disturbing—so they need careful planning. Here, the contrast between the black and white is offset by the soft yellow, and the room is lightened by an off-white ceiling and fireplace surround, and neutral buff color on the floor. In this type of scheme there is no need for color accents to add interest; instead, neutrals are used as a calming influence. Other strong contrasts come from complementary colors, which lie opposite each other on the color wheel.

ARCAID / GEOFF LUNG

■ If you are at a loss for inspiration as you plan to decorate a room or are not sure how your favorite colors will look together, make up a sample board, as shown on page 6. Take a piece of cardboard and stick onto it samples of the paints, papers, fabrics or carpets that you want to use, laying them out as they would appear, with the carpet at the bottom, and so on. Show each element in the proportion in which it will finally appear—small strips of paint color for baseboard or chair rails and large areas for walls and ceilings. This will give you a preview of the overall look and allow you to try out alternatives until you get it right. Once you have decided on a color scheme and are ready to choose wallpapers and paints, remember to look at samples holding them vertically, as they will appear on your walls. Paint samples always look much lighter when you see them on a horizontal plane, but if you hold a paint chart vertically, the colors will immediately look darker. By selecting a paint just one shade lighter than the one you first chose, you can avoid a costly mistake and be sure that the finished effect will be just as you planned.

3

The color wheel

The color wheel, opposite, is a graduated spectrum of color and is a standard means of defining and describing color. It is built around the three primary colors, which are red, blue and yellow.

If you mix pairs of primary colors together in equal proportions, you get the three secondary colors—red and yellow make orange, red and blue create violet or purple, and blue mixed with yellow makes green.

When these secondary colors are mixed with the primary color next to them on the wheel, they make the six tertiary colors—red and orange make red-orange; red and violet make red-violet;

blue and violet make blue-violet; blue and green, blue-green; yellow and green, yellow-green; yellow and orange, yellow-orange—and this completes the circle.

Tints and tones

If you have ever been faced with the possibilities of color within one range of paint, fabric, wallcovering or flooring, you will know that every color has varieties of tone. Adding white to a color makes a tint, adding black gives a shade of the original color and adding gray to a color makes a midtone.

When planning a color scheme, it is important to get a balance between these color

values. If all your colors are pale tints, the room's overall appearance will be weak and anemic; a color scheme composed only of midtones will be monotonous; and a room decorated only in dark

shades will be dark and feel very gloomy.

Warm and cool

The color wheel divides naturally across the middle. On one side are warm colors—red, orange, yellow, pink, apricot, peach, terra-cotta, gold, warm browns, tans, plums, some warm purples and lilacs. These warm, or advancing, colors seem to come toward you and make a space seem smaller—so you can use them to make a feature stand out or to create a warm, cozy atmosphere.

On the opposite side are cool, or receding, colors—blue, green, jade, turquoise, mint, yellow-green, greenish gold, blue-lilacs and cool purples. These seem to go away from you, so they can make a room look larger and create a spacious feel. Too many warm colors in strong values can be claustrophobic, and too many cool colors can be chilly, so you need to get a balance of the two. Use neutral colors—black, white, gray and beige—to soften or add emphasis and achieve a harmonious effect.

Natural inspirations

The lushest colors on paint charts and swatches are often named after natural inspirations—raspberry pink, buttercup, midnight blue, leaf green or fuchsia. Nature is full of wonderful color combinations—dazzling schemes that, although often are unexpected, never jar or look uncomfortable against each other. In a natural monochromatic color scheme, the green shades of a forest sit comfortably next to each other

and are accented by the soft browns of ferns and foliage. Similarly, the natural colors of wicker and straw combine the "friendly" colors in the brown-to-yellow section of the color wheel to create a scheme of related colors. For one of nature's starkest contrasts, look at the center of the petals of a tulip, below. The vibrant yellow and shining black look dazzling together; and in just the same way, a room scheme that uses these colors together is stimulating to the eye and full of energy.

THE IMAGE BANK

ROBERT HARDING PICTURE LIBRARY

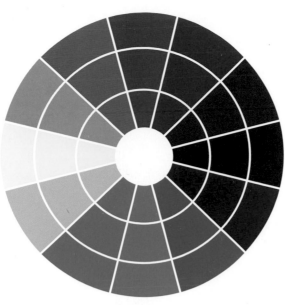

▼ TINTS

If you add white to a pure color you make a tint. All the colors in the wheel below are tints, with increasing amounts of white to lighten them.

▲ THE COLOR WHEEL

Above, the graduated spectrum shows all the primary, secondary and tertiary colors in their full strengths, undiluted with white or black.

▼ SHADES

If you add black to a pure color, the result is a shade. The wheel below shows how increasing the amount of black darkens the colors to create a new range of deeper hues.

Color theory

The basics of color theory are a reliable way of ensuring that any color scheme you plan will work well.

ROOM SIZE

Bright, deep, strong and contrasting colors tend to look twice as bold when used over a large area, as will large or jazzy patterns. These "advance," like warm colors, whereas pale colors and small patterns look lighter in large areas and tend to recede. Always relate the strength of a color and the scale of a pattern to the size of the area in which you want to use it.

BOLD COLORS

If you stare hard at a strong color, you will find that when you look away you can see an after-image in the color that is its direct opposite on the color wheel. This is a natural reaction by the eye, but can be very useful in planning contrasting schemes.

SPLIT SCHEMES

By combining a main color with the two colors on either side of its direct opposite on the color wheel, you get a split complementary scheme, which has all the visual stimulus of a complementary combination. Add variety by using accents in different tints, tones and shades.

Color planning

Generally, color schemes can be divided into three main groups: monochromatic schemes; neighborly, or related, harmonies; and contrasting, or complementary, combinations.

Monochromatic schemes

The colors for this sort of scheme should come from just one segment of the wheel, with no wavering to either side. Build up a scheme using different strengths of your chosen color and add all-important tonal variety with accessories (or accents) in contrasting colors or neutrals.

Related harmonies

These schemes are built up using colors from three or four adjacent sections on the color wheel. The art here is to balance the warm and cool colors; so if all your colors are either warm or cool, add accents from the other side of the wheel. If your range of colors includes both warm and cool colors, add accents in neutrals.

Complementary colors

The colors opposite each other on the wheel are called *complementary colors* and together can create some very effective schemes. By definition, such schemes bring together warm and cool colors, which naturally complement each other. But because warm colors tend to advance, these colors will tend to dominate a scheme, so for a 50/50 effect, use only one-third of the warm color to two-thirds of the cool one. If in doubt, use the pale and midtones for the main room surfaces and keep the stronger ones for accents.

Monochrome

Green is generally considered a cool color, but the slightly yellow tinge to the green in this bathroom and the use of yellow and a warm, pinky mauve in the highlights make it warmer, without affecting the sense of space that cool colors create. Clever use of light yellow-green on the angled wall prevents it from looking closed in.

Related harmony

Beiges and creams are sometimes classed as neutrals, but they are really an extension of the range of browns and yellows. These related colors make a room very peaceful, and because of their closeness to neutral white, they give an open, spacious feel— which makes this an ideal scheme to use when decorating smaller rooms.

Color contrast

White is a warm neutral, and black a cool one, so the combination on the tartan rug and upholstery is tempered with soft yellow and plain white. Busy, contrasting patterns, such as tartan, are best used in moderation, even in larger rooms, or they can become dominant and make a room feel small or claustrophobic.

Upholstery

The fabric you select for upholstery or, in the case of a bathroom, for the towels or bath mat, is an integral part of the color scheme. Take advantage of the service offered by most interior design companies and take home good-sized samples to help you to match colors accurately.

Details

Add details that contribute to the atmosphere of your room. Starfish and "sunken treasure," such as this sea-horse handled urn, give an aquatic feel to a bathroom.

Color theory

The fixtures in a bathroom are just as much a part of the color scheme as the walls and floor, and they are likely to be the most expensive or difficult element to change. Build up a scheme around the color of the fixtures, or in the case of a kitchen, the worktops and cabinets.

Accessories

Use colorful accessories to accent your color scheme: Ceramic pots, vases and ornaments all contribute to the overall look of a room, adding color or giving a particular style. These glazed earthenware crocks are perfect in a room of terra-cottas and creams.
If possible, choose your floorcovering first, then build up the scheme around it, lightening or darkening the room with the wall color. A richly colored rug can make a large, light-colored floor more cozy.

Color theory

Choose a color for painting the baseboard, doors, window frames and other woodwork. If you have radiators, unless you particularly want to make a feature of them, paint them in a color to blend with the walls where they stand so that they blend with the background and do not stand out.

ALL ACCESSORIES PHOTOS: ROBERT HARDING PICTURE LIBRARY

Extend the look

If your furniture has a distinctive look like the elegant black metal chairs in this room, it can look very effective if you echo the colors and style in pottery or decorative items. Although it would be too expensive to change your accessories every time you redecorated, a few ornamental items or flowers—in colors that either blend or contrast with the main scheme—can extend the look of room.

Color theory

In a "quiet" color scheme, you might be adventurous with a colored ceiling; but if the rest of the room is decorated in vibrant and contrasting colors, choose white or a very pale ceiling color to give the room a feeling of height. A dark ceiling makes a room seem less spacious.

7

Creams and golds

Look to nature for inspiration, such as the sandy colors of desert dunes and the sky. Or combine the soft golds, yellows and creamy whites of daffodils, narcissus and sweet peas, adding contrasting accents in pale sky blue to add variety and interest.

Use a group of neighborly colors from the color wheel to create relaxed, comfortable room schemes that are easy to live with. These versatile color combinations can create any atmosphere you choose and suit any size, shape and style of room.

COLOR harmony

Blue-greens

Decorate a warm kitchen in blues and greens, using different tones of these colors to create interest. Add warm accents to prevent the scheme from being too cold without destroying the harmony.

Yellow-greens

Harmonious schemes can create a feeling of cohesion in link areas, such as a hall. Use grassy yellow-greens for a hall that leads into a garden to give a comfortable flow of colors between one area and another.

Color theory

■ Harmonious, relaxing color schemes, which use related colors, are the easiest to live with. Cool schemes can be calming, while warm ones are welcoming. Contrasting, or clashing, colors can help to create a stimulating, busy atmosphere. Relate your choice to the way you propose to use the room—its basic style, size and shape, the direction it faces, and the amount of natural daylight it receives.

■ Cool harmonious schemes will help to create an impression of space as well as a calm atmosphere. Warm neighborly colors feel cozy, but take care not to let them become too enclosing. To avoid this, choose midtone and pale values of the colors. If you prefer to mix the two types of color in a room without causing too much contrast, then base the scheme on no more than four adjacent segments on the color wheel.

■ Adjacent color schemes can create a feeling of harmony, especially in a small apartment, condo or house, where linked color schemes will create an impression of greater space. Such schemes also work well where two rooms open into or adjoin each other, and you want the scheme to flow from one room to the next to create visual unity.

S ometimes it is difficult to decide which colors to use together, but if you choose related, or harmonious, colors (sometimes called analogous colors), you can be sure that they will work well together. These are the neighborly colors, next to each other on the color wheel (see Color Know-how, page 5).

It is up to you how large a segment of the wheel you select: You can use two, three, four or even five sections. These can be all cool—the blue-lilacs, blues, blue-greens and greens—or all warm—reds or pinks, red-orange, terra-cottas,

peaches, apricots and sunny yellows; or a mixture of both types of color. If you stick to all one type, the result will be more harmonious than if you use both warm and cool colors together.

Tonal balance

For a successful scheme, aim to achieve a tonal balance—this means mixing rich dark shades with midtones and some pale tints, then using a neutral, such as white, cream or gray, to act as a link or contrast. This will add interest without using strong, disturbing contrasts. Remember to

A richly colored terra-cotta stone floor ▶ provides a base for the color scheme in this peach, brown and cream kitchen. The warmth of the scheme is enhanced by the use of a soft apricot color for the ceiling, and cooling accents are added in the form of plants, greenery and the white surfaces.

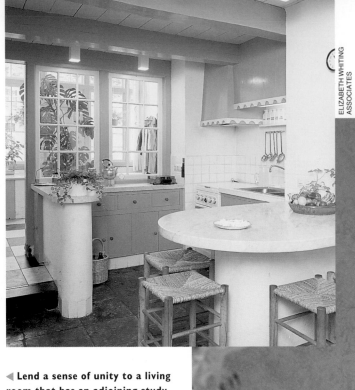

◀ Lend a sense of unity to a living room that has an adjoining study or dining area by extending the carpeting throughout both rooms and echoing the overall scheme of warm woody colors, soft yellows and golds. Similar rugs in both rooms emphasize the feeling of coordination and space.

Greens and yellows ▲ create a dining room that is easy on the eye— a place to enjoy leisurely meals and relax over after-dinner drinks. The collection of colored glasses adds interest and crisp texture to a softly aged wooden cupboard.

contrast textures of surfaces, too—some shiny, others flat or matte, several light-absorbing and a few light-filtering—to give depth to the scheme. This is vital when the scheme relies for effect on tonal contrasts of one main color only.

If you want to create a warm, harmonious scheme—for instance, to brighten up a cold bathroom—you could work up a scheme using very pale yellow tiles on the walls and a slightly paler tone of yellow paint on the ceiling. Choose a cheerful fabric, striped in yellow, apricot, peach and terra-cotta on a neutral white or cream background, for the window treatment and paint the woodwork white or cream and the floor in terra-

cotta. Add towels in golds, yellows, apricot, peach and terra-cotta with a little olive green as an accent to add more visual interest.

Working with color groups

In an east-facing bedroom, combine a deep rose carpet with pale lilac-pink walls, a blue ceiling and white woodwork. The curtains and bed linen could be patterned in pinks, magenta, lilacs, purples and deep blue on white to tie the scheme together. Pinks, lilac-pinks. mauves, blue-lilacs and blue work particularly harmoniously in this type of scheme.

To create a country-style living room, use

ARCAID: KEN KIRKWOOD. INSET, ABODE UK

▲ The yellow-to-blue side of the color wheel provides the basis for this cleverly decorated living room. The two tones of yellow on the walls give a soft tiled effect, achieved by using a small roller, and the trompe l'oeil shutters give the impression of a country-style room.

◄ Predominantly pink but tending toward the yellow side of the color wheel, this cottage living room has a warm atmosphere, made even more cozy by the enclosing effect of wood beams on the ceiling. Neutral cream or white is almost always a safe choice as a background for harmonious color schemes such as this.

terra-cotta tiles or carpet for the floor; peach walls and ceiling; deep gold upholstery; and chintz curtains with a floral pattern in pale sunny yellow, rich burnt-orange, olive and spring greens on an off-white background. Echo these colors in accessories and link the scheme together with creamy off-whites and neutrals.

For a feeling of space, blend the curtains in with the walls. This is where coordinated, or companion, fabrics and wallcoverings can be used to great effect. Just remember to measure carefully and ensure that any patterns line up across the surfaces.

You can also use a harmonious scheme to do

the opposite and make a large area appear more intimate. Use the warmer neighborly colors for the main surfaces, contrasted with a cool color. You could go around the wheel from red-orange, orange, yellow-orange and yellow, through to the yellow-greens. Use Indian reds, terra-cottas and golds with pale creamy yellows for the main surfaces and accents in lime green.

For a cozy look, start at red and work through warm red-violets to blue-violet contrasts. Try an Oriental rug in plummy reds and deep purple-blue with mahogany-stained floorboards. Use a deep red wallcovering, or a self-stripe, if the room is low-ceilinged, and echo this in accessories.

Creams and golds

ELIZABETH WHITING ASSOCIATES

The main impression of this room is of one schemed around creamy yellows and blue—but the blue is mainly an accent color. The main wall surfaces and furniture are based on a harmonious mixture of creams, yellows and browns, which create a warm and mellow atmosphere. Highlights in blue and white add texture, pattern and interest to the overall scheme of the room.

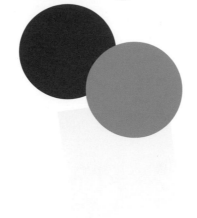

Cool down a bright or sunny scheme with accents in a cool color, such as blue.

PHOTOGRAPHY BY DAVE KING

Blue-greens

ROBERT HARDING PICTURE LIBRARY

A scheme using a mixture of plain greens and blues is given visual interest and texture by the addition of checked and plaid accessories, curtains and table linen. This texture still echoes the main color scheme, but includes a deep red color that is picked up by the flowers and details in the paintwork. This touch of color saves the room from looking too blue and cool.

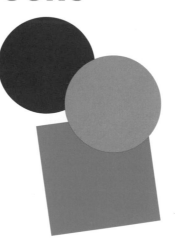

Colors from the cool side of the color wheel need accents in a warm color.

Yellow-greens

ABODE UK

Yellows, greens and a few touches of blue are combined to give a mellow and subtle effect. The woodwork, walls and window areas are all gently distressed, linking them to the overall feeling of rustic elegance. Hand-painted vines around the doorway and window frames add just the right level of additional color and detail to the scheme.

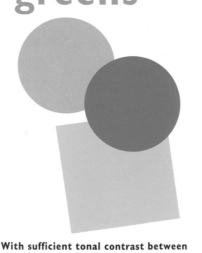

With sufficient tonal contrast between harmonious colors, few accents are necessary.

Warm and cool colors

When you choose the accent colors to balance the warm and cool elements in a color scheme, make sure you know what effect large areas of upholstery are going to have on the overall feel of the room. A pure, light blue, such as the sofa, below, or the pottery on the right, will add a cool element to a sunny room, whereas a greenish blue would tend to create an aquatic look.

ALL ACCESSORIES : ROBERT HARDING PICTURE LIBRARY

Color theory

Use a paler value of the main color for the walls (either paint or washable wallcovering in well-used areas). Choose the lightest color for the ceiling and/or the woodwork. Accent colors can be used to pick out and make a feature of chair or dado rails, or to add interest in the form of decorative borders.

Textured details

The reflective qualities of colored glass, the patterned interest of decorated porcelain and interestingly shaped frames in toning colors will add visual impact to a harmonious scheme.

Color theory

For a relaxing and calm atmosphere, one of the most successful and harmonious schemes is a monochromatic or tone-on-tone one, based on different values of one color. These schemes are easy to create, especially if you use paint manufacturers' color cards. Each card is a monochromatic scheme in itself, so you can use these as a guide.

Faded elegance

A room schemed in distressed greens and golden yellows needs mellow furniture, such as the wicker chair on the right; or in the case of a dining room, a soft, toning fabric, such as damask, and accents in the form of green glass and touches of muted gilding.

Use foliage, such as ivy, to add a natural accent in keeping with the elegant, almost rustic look.

Color theory

Yellows and greens are fresh, warm colors, ideal for creating a welcoming atmosphere in a foyer or a reception room. Add plants in which these colors are most prominent to add a softening touch to rooms that seem cool or slightly stark.

13

COLOR &SP

Lack of space is a common problem with many houses, condos and apartments. Small rooms often have no natural light or they are awkwardly shaped. This is where some clever tricks with color can create an impression of space.

Ceiling treatments

In a small room, one of the best ways to increase the apparent height of a low or sloping ceiling is to paint the ceiling to match the walls or, perhaps, a shade lighter than the walls. Also, you could paper the ceiling to match the walls. If you paper the ceiling, make sure that the wallpaper design is nondirectional; otherwise, it might be difficult to match patterns at the join between the walls and ceiling.

ACE

ROBERT HARDING PICTURE LIBRARY. INSET: THE IMAGE BANK

THE PHOTOGRAPHERS LIBRARY. INSET: THE IMAGE BANK

Color theory

■ Contrary to popular belief, white rooms can look very dazzling and uninviting—and may not look spacious at all. A warm color, however, such as a very pale yellow, with a high reflectance value, may be more successful.

■ Light-filtering textures, such as slatted blinds and open-weave fabrics—lace, nets, muslin, voile—as well as cane and wickerwork, trellis and glass, all tend to diffuse and soften the light, creating an impression that the room is larger than it actually is.

■ If you do not like the cooler range of colors, or if the room is already cold and possibly dark, then use the paler values of the warmer colors—pinks, peaches, apricots, soft yellows. A monochromatic effect will help to magnify the apparent size of the area. And a neutral scheme based on cream, taupes, subtle beiges, soft browns and caramels will create space without being enclosing.

Corner rooms

Soft, neutral colors make the most of a space, no matter how small or oddly shaped. Avoid bold patterns, heavy furniture, oversized accessories and contrasting colors. Instead, add small decorations, such as accessories in toning colors on light glass shelves. The sandy contours of desert dunes, left, are a perfect example of the way natural light and shade and soft, neutral colors create the impression of space.

Enhancing space

If you want to make any room look more spacious, avoid strong color contrasts and clashing designs. Choose upholstery in colors that echo the floor treatment or with the same strength of color. Above, the muted tones of a rocky canyon create a sense of space and light, as well as a feeling of warmth.

R ooms are rarely perfectly proportioned, but there is no need to feel cramped or claustrophobic in small or oddly shaped rooms. Some crafty camouflage tricks can create a sense of openness and sunshine.

Cool, receding colors and pale tones, such as soft blues, greens and silver grays, all help to create an impression of greater space. Monochromatic and restrained neutral schemes will also have this effect, although all these may look chilly and dull unless you use them with flair.

Patterns can also contribute to an impression of space. Avoid strong designs on major surfaces and instead use small-print patterns, simple geometric motifs or soft-focus florals. Designs printed with one color on a neutral ground are a good compromise between patterns and plains.

Floors and carpets

The floor is one of the bigger, unbroken areas of a room, so if you can enlarge this visually, you will immediately create an impression of greater

A color scheme based on the paler values of the ▶
cool, receding colors—the blues, greens, silver
grays—will create a spacious impression in any room.
Glass shelves, fixed across a window (provided the
window is not to be opened) and used to display
plants or colored glass objects, can also be effective
in creating an impression of space.

Creating illusions

USING PATTERNS

Vertical stripes on walls, tongue-and-groove
paneling or beadboard paneling will all carry
the eye upward. Similarly, stripes for curtains
or blinds at the windows, or vertical venetian
blinds, will also help to create an impression of
added height.

USING TEXTURES

Texture can be used to create an impression of
greater space. Painted surfaces with a gloss
finish, shiny ceramic tiles, foil and silky-
textured wallcoverings all reflect the light.
Chintz, satin and silk fabrics and metallics,
such as brass, silver, chrome and stainless
steel—even laminates, mirrors and varnished
or polished wood—suggest a feeling of space,
because of the way they deflect the light.

ROBERT HARDING PICTURE LIBRARY

◀ In a very small
apartment, house or
cottage, plan the
scheme so that the
colors flow from area to
area, and there are no
jarring effects when
doors are open. This will
create an overall
impression of space—
especially if you use
light, toning or
neutral colors.

space. Avoid very strong colors or boldly
patterned rugs and carpets, and don't break up
the floor with too many different treatments.
Decorate walls in a slightly paler value, but in the
same basic color as the floor: Try sponging,
stippling, dragging or marbling, using the floor
color as the base with a slightly paler top coat.

Try to use the same floorcovering throughout a
small property, as this carries the eye through
into the next space, increasing the apparent size.
Otherwise, use the same color or tonal value for
all the floors, or pick a simple, patterned carpet in
several colors for the hall, stairs and landing, and
echo each color in the rooms leading off.

When planning color schemes for small rooms,

THE PHOTOGRAPHERS LIBRARY

ELIZABETH WHITING ASSOCIATES

◄ It can be hard to make a large room look warm and inviting. Here, the detailing on the ceiling and the blue paintwork on the coving and baseboard break the impression of size. Rich, dark colors and side lighting give a much needed feeling of intimacy.

▼ Too much space can be as tricky a problem as too little space. Break up a large room by cornering off a cozy area with a couch, coffee table and chairs, as below, and bring in the walls by hanging generously sized pictures and painting the woodwork in a different color from the walls so that it does not blend in.

ELIZABETH WHITING ASSOCIATES

ROBERT HARDING PICTURE LIBRARY

USING LIGHT

In the daytime, natural light coming into a room—and being reflected back from a light-reflecting surface—helps create an illusion of greater space. Keep window treatments simple (roller blinds cut out very little light), and hang curtains on poles that extend well past the edge of the window frame, so that they can be drawn right back to the sides of the window during the day.

MIRRORS

In a very small room or a tiny hall or a narrow corridor, cleverly placed mirrors will help you to expand the size visually. The effect will be further enhanced if you position the mirror where it will reflect light—either from a window or an artificial source inside. A fake window made with a framed mirror in a windowless bathroom can be very effective—try adding some small curtains or a blind to increase the illusion.

MIRROR TILES

A wall of mirror tiles can be very effective, doubling the impression of space in a small room, such as a bathroom. Make sure, however, that the walls are completely smooth and flat; uneven surfaces covered with mirror tiles can create very disturbing distorted images.

try to create visual unity. This does not mean all the rooms have to be boringly similar—use a similar color palette but in different designs and textures. For example, you might hang the main design of a wallcovering in the living room, using the companion fabric for curtains. Use a simpler, coordinating wallcovering in the dining room, with blinds edged with a fabric border to echo the living room curtains, thus creating a calming uniformity.

Camouflage

Keep wall treatments simple and blend window treatments into the background so that the wall is not a visual distraction. Choose uncomplicated curtains with no swags, tails, frills or flounces, or neatly tailored blinds in a similar color and/or pattern to the wall treatment.

Treat features, such as built-in furniture, fireplaces and radiators, to match the walls so that they also fade into the background, or color them so that they become an integral part of the scheme. Sometimes a complete camouflage treatment can be very successful with a design, such as a cloudscape, a rainbow or an underwater scene, painted across both walls and furniture.

One of the most effective ways of dealing with small spaces and low ceilings is to use the trompe l'oeil trick and paint a vista that suggests endless sky and distant views.

Monochrome

Your choice of colors will be most effective in enhancing a small or awkwardly shaped space if you you use a monochromatic treatment, basing the whole room on different tones of one color. Use a midtone for the floor, with paler values for the walls and ceiling; then, as in this room, add some color accents in the painted woodwork around the window frames.

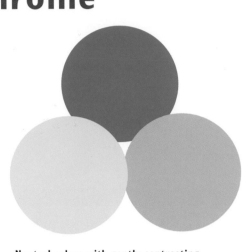

Neutral colors with gently contrasting highlights make the most of small spaces.

Cool greens

The pale tones that give a floor the best impression of space are not always practical. Instead, use floor tiles in a checkerboard pattern, picking out the lighter tile color for the baseboard, coving and other paintwork. Green can be cool or warm; this forest green shade is cool and receding, so although the walls are quite a deep shade of green, the overall effect is of calm and space.

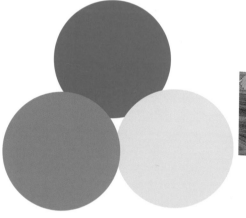

Shades of green with highlights of sandy yellow look cool and easy on the eye.

Peach tones

If you want to enhance the sense of space in a room, avoid strong or really bright hues or primary colors for main surfaces. Use subtle, grayed values—Indian reds, subtle gray-greens or, as in the room on the left, roses and blue-grays. If you use mainly paler tones for a room scheme, introduce deeper tonal values in smaller areas or as accents.

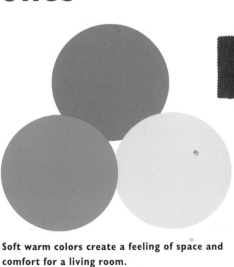

Soft warm colors create a feeling of space and comfort for a living room.

Echo the colors of any accents in the room with suitably proportioned ornaments or accessories on the walls or shelves, but avoid heavy-looking cabinets in which to display them.

Color theory

If you find one-color and neutral schemes too plain, then use neighborly colors that are adjacent on a color wheel. Although they provide more color interest than mono-chromatic schemes, they are not as stimulating as the contrasting or complementary ones.

Choosing furniture

Make sure that you choose furniture that is in proportion to the size of the room and that is not dominant or cluttering. Slim wooden dining chairs or neat, unfussy armchairs are ideal.

Neighborly colors

Shades of green, yellow and cream—colors adjacent on the color wheel—create a look that is easy on the eye. If you want to use several colors for accessories in a small room, such a scheme is ideal.

Color theory

Although large leafy plants can take up a lot of space in a room, the cool, receding green of the foliage and the softening effect this has on the contours of a room mean that plants tend to enhance the impression of space. Choose species with elegantly shaped leaves that break up the light—another ploy to give a feeling of greater space.

Peaches and blues

Choose furniture that blends with the main color scheme. Avoid thick, heavy pieces and choose instead small, dainty chairs, tables, cabinets and paintings or prints that blend in comfortably.

Color theory

Windows are a vital element in giving a room a feeling of light and space. If there is little natural light available, enhance what there is by using mirrors. When hanging these, remember to check that the reflection does not draw attention to any unsightly views before finalizing the position.

The softening effect of wood wash in a toning color is ideal for making a solid-looking piece of furniture, such as a small corner cabinet, look less dominant.

Cool and relaxing

The combination of chrome and pale apple green creates a cool, tranquil environment in this bathroom. The skylight is the main light source, and opaque glass helps to filter what would otherwise be dazzling sunlight in the summer. Just as textures in the quiltlike pattern of the countryside (inset) complement each other, the textured rug and matte walls are good foils for the many reflective surfaces.

Our perception of colors depends entirely on the light in which we view them, so the same color can look vibrant or dingy in different lighting. Find out how to choose the right colors for your lighting and how to make the most of a poorly lit room.

COLOR
and li

When you are planning a new room scheme, first assess the quality of the natural daylight in the room. Light plays tricks with colors, so the same shade of yellow can look vivid and brilliant in sunlight or dreary and muddy in a poorly lit space. Consider the time of day you most often use the room, but take note of the light throughout the day. Ideally, you need to take account of the seasons, too.

Light influences

Rooms that face north tend to have a clear, rather clinical light, which is usually the best for true color rendition. (This is why most artists' studios have large north-facing windows.) But this type of light can make a room feel very cold and stark; white in such a room gives a harsh, drab appearance. South-facing rooms are usually the opposite; they have a warmer, softer natural light and usually suit clear, bright colors.

East-facing rooms get the light in the mornings but tend to be rather gloomy in the afternoons and evenings. These ▶

Natural look

The neutrality of this scheme gives an overall feeling of light. Too much extra natural light would make the room cold and stark, so this scheme would suit a south-facing room. Draped muslin acts as a filter, while the picture and the glass-topped table both reflect effectively.

Two-tone bathroom

Sometimes unexpected color combinations work well in the unlikeliest of places, as this ocher and purple bathroom demonstrates. The jeweled light shade casts multicolored lights over the room, which the brass fittings reflect to some degree. There is no source of natural light in the room, which is why the striking color scheme works; too much sunlight would make the colors look garish and incompatible.

ght

Color theory

■ The quality of light changes dramatically with different latitudes and can result in regional color preferences. For example, in sunny Florida, houses are often painted pink and other pastel shades, which would look garish in a cold, gray climate.

■ In the southwest, strong but mellow daylight makes the most of earthy terra-cottas and ochers and deep azure and turquoise blues. They shine and reflect the light to spectacular effect, but would look overpowering on houses in the clearer northeastern light.

■ In northern Europe, where cloud cover creates a gray haze, muted, warm colors are popular. In Sweden, which only has a few hours of daylight in winter, houses are often painted blue and yellow to suggest sky and sunshine, or green, to suggest the grass and trees which are hidden by snow.

■ Texture affects the way light strikes a surface and is then absorbed, reflected or filtered. This, in turn, alters the way color is perceived. Two differently textured fabrics, colored with the same pigments, will look different. This is why lighting conditions and texture should be carefully considered when color-matching.

Two effective and ▲
attractive ways of
filtering light are using
leafy fronds and hanging
ornaments in the window
(top) or choosing stained
glass in muted colors
(above).

rooms need colors and textures to warm them up later in the day. Most west-facing rooms have a warm glow in the evenings and can take cooler tones, with warm accents to prevent a morning chill.

Textural balance

It is always important to achieve a textural balance as well as tonal contrast in a room. If all the surfaces are similar, the result will be rather one-dimensional, even if the textures are varied. Try to combine pale, mid and dark color strengths (or values) in equal proportions. The colors can vary, too, unless you have decided to try out a monochromatic scheme.

A color scheme using all shiny surfaces can be stimulating, dazzling or even disturbing; one with mainly rough or matte finishes may be dull and potentially suffocating, because most of the light is absorbed by the walls, floor and furniture. Too many light-filtering textures tend to create a wishy-washy, ethereal effect, lacking in stability. A successful scheme needs a combination of all

three types of texture, as well as different colors or color values.

Glass can add a light and effective contrast to a heavy scheme. A glass-topped table will make a room seem more spacious, whereas a group of leafy green plants lit by a floor-mounted uplight underneath the table will create a clean but warming glow. You can achieve a similar effect if you choose glass-fronted display cabinets illuminated with integral lighting.

Try teaming plush velvets with colored, backlit glass and large mirrors. Smooth velvet will reflect light, as will the mirrors, but the colored glass will cast a cozy, mystical glow over the room.

Simple colored-glass bottles, vases and other accessories placed on shelves or on a windowsill where the light can shine through them or stained-glass panels, throwing pools of colored light onto the floor, walls or ceiling, will all create a jewel-like effect in a plain room. This makes good use of natural daylight and can be combined with lamps and candles for a night-time glow. Cornice lighting above a window will simulate natural light.

ROBERT HARDING PICTURE LIBRARY/BRIAN HARRISON (TOP)

Color theory

■ A small, sunless living room can be visually enlarged by the use of pale, cool colors and suitable textures. Soft creams and terra-cottas, combined with ocher, black and touches of green, will add space, light and height. A mixture of jazzy patterns and more conservative stripes adds points of interest to what could otherwise become too plain a scheme.

■ If you have a dark basement, a cold kitchen or a long, gloomy hallway, you can immediately improve things by using light, sunny colors (yellows, warm pinks, terra-cottas, pale tangerines and creams) with shiny surfaces for extra reflection. In a gloomy bedroom, for example, try a brass bedstead and white laminated built-in furniture with brass trim; a pale sky blue ceiling, in satin or mid-sheen paint; a deep gold carpet; peach, blue and yellow silk-textured wallcoverings and brocade curtains.

■ In a small bathroom that has tiny, opaque windows, gleaming fixtures and polished tiles and mirrors will help to reflect light. Combine these textures with pale, warm colors and the room will seem larger, warmer and more welcoming. Add rugs or wall hangings for texture.

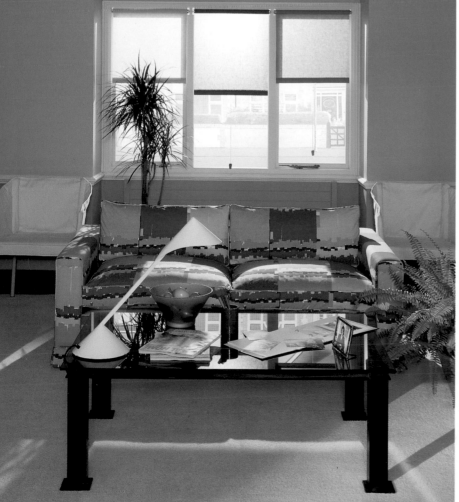

▲ Small rooms that do not benefit from much sunlight look larger decorated in cool, pale colors. Add a little warm light—try a yellow or peach light bulb with a neutral shade—to prevent the room from looking bare or dull. Choose accessories in earthy tones, such as this ethnic wall hanging, to cheer things up.

◄ The trick is to match color schemes to the type of light your room enjoys. So if your living room is generally sunny, like this one, you can afford to choose vibrant Mediterranean colors, while a north-facing room will suit more subtle shades.

23

Creams and pine

Cream, white and pine blend beautifully to give a fresh, Scandinavian feel. The wood warms up what could otherwise be a rather uninviting scheme, and fresh flowers have the perfect backdrop of wispy muslin and natural light. Different shades of cream and white work well together. Soften the look and add texture with delicate, lacy fabrics and a neutral checkerboard carpet.

Soft tones and light-reflecting colors enhance the feeling of space in a room.

Fern greens

Pale green is known for its relaxing effect and works well whatever the size of your bathroom. These traditional white fixtures with chrome fittings give the bathroom a clean, highly polished look. Suspended globe lights echo the white porcelain and act as light reflectors. A huge potted palm and a large display of blowsy blooms prevent the room from looking too clinical.

Greens can be cool or warm—accessorize to warm in winter and cool in summer.

Purples and ochers

The combination of deep purple and rich ocher gives this bathroom an almost gothic feel, and the ornate brass shelf and toning accessories add to the aged look. Striking combinations like this work surprisingly well in darker rooms, where lighter colors could look dingy. The jeweled light shade adds a hint of dramatic glamour as well as drawing the eye toward the skylight.

Take complementary colors from the color wheel for successful bold color schemes.

Warm touch

A predominantly white or cream room needs something to draw the eye and add warmth. This wicker chair is perfect for a bedroom, and the cushion can be covered in a light floral or in delicate lace. Cream wallpaper with gold detail, lit by glass-shaded lamps, adds a cozy glow.

ROBERT HARDING PICTURE LIBRARY/CLIFFORD JONES (LEFT)/MICHAEL DUNNE (RIGHT)

Color theory

A color scheme based on different values of one color makes a room seem bigger. Try teaming champagne-colored furniture with cream-colored walls and ceiling, champagne-and-white tiles with a peaches-and-cream border, or champagne-and-white striped blinds with bronze-and-cream checkerboard tiles or flooring.

Light reflectors

Apple green looks wonderful next to white. In a large bathroom, you can afford to choose unusual accessories, such as this painted birdcage. Large rooms with only one main light source need shiny accessories to reflect the light elsewhere. This chrome bathroom cart is a strong focal point, and the rounded structure would soften the look of angular cabinets.

ROBERT HARDING PICTURE LIBRARY (LEFT AND RIGHT)/MADELEINE REES (LEFT ONLY)

Color theory

If you do choose a monochromatic scheme, it's important to add some points of contrast in your accessories. For example, if your bedroom or living room is predominantly green, add a strikingly colored vase, an embroidered pillow, an eye-catching painting, a flowering houseplant or just a spray of fresh flowers.

Bold and gothic

If you like the strong colors of the two-tone bathroom, you will probably enjoy dramatic accessories, too. This copperleaf and collage frame would make a good surround for a gothic-looking bathroom mirror, and the stylish copper shaving mirror and accessories set has interesting lines, which draw the eye.

ROBERT HARDING PICTURE LIBRARY/JO SCHOFIELD (LEFT)/TREVOR RICHARDS (RIGHT)

Color theory

In a dark room, there are two possible strategies. One is to choose a cozy, rich scheme with warm but strongly contrasting colors; the other is to get as much light in as possible, using pale, sunny colors and light-reflecting textures, such as glass, onyx, mirrors and veneered woods.

Bold
CONTRASTS

The clever use of contrasting colors can lend a room character and interest. Discover how to combine opposite colors and contrasting shades for the most pleasing effects.

Some of the most successful color schemes rely on contrast for their impact—and this does not have to come from the major surfaces in the room. You can emphasize the main color theme of a room by the clever addition of contrasting accents and accessories—it is a subtle and inexpensive way of introducing seasonal changes into a room, adding warm accents in winter and cooler ones in summer.

Contrast can come in many combinations. You can set light against a dark background or use warm colors to accent a cold scheme, or vice versa. Or you can combine pure colors with subtle tones or use strong accents to brighten up a neutral look or a tone-on-tone look.

ROBERT HARDING PICTURE LIBRARY. INSET: THE IMAGE BANK

ELIZABETH WHITING ASSOCIATES. INSET: THE IMAGE BANK

Deep pink and yellow

This daring yet successful combination of bright floral colors uses two shades from the warm side of the color wheel. Natural fiber flooring, wood and wicker furniture and cooling touches of green in the upholstery and the foliage tone down the brightness of the scheme.

Mauve, blue and green

The rich Mediterranean blue of the table supplies a strong contrast with the softer mauve of the cupboards and the deep green of the table legs. Although all the colors come from the cool side of the color wheel, the contrast in shades, even between related colors, makes a striking impression.

■ The best way to achieve bold contrasts that are exciting to the eye yet comfortable to live with is to base the main scheme on complementary colors. These are colors that lie opposite each other on the color wheel (see Color Know-how, page 2). By doing this, you can strike a compromise between a scheme that is too bright and brash, and finding yourself restricted to adding color interest only in the form of accessories.

You do not need to use colors at their strongest values, but it is a good idea to introduce some contrast of tone. For instance, you might use fresh spring green with deep Indian red, or candy pink with bright emerald green. Combine glowing gold with lilac, or lemon with deep purple; set apricot against a deep navy blue, or terracotta against turquoise. But remember, a warm color will always appear more dominant than a cool one, so whatever you use it for—fabric, floor or furniture—will stand out noticeably. Take care to get the balance of hot and cold in a room just right.

Rich red and blue

The matte maroon red of the upper walls has almost the rusty look of sandstone, inset, in its duskiness. Although primary red and blue could look overpowering together, these two darkened shades give this study a warm and comfortable atmosphere.

Patterns can be equally effective. Set off bright jazzy patterns against a plain background, or use plain fabrics or wallcoverings to link or tone down a heavily patterned scheme.

Complementary contrasts

Generally, schemes that rely on strong color contrasts are highly stimulating, so they are not first choice for rooms where the mood needs to be relaxing—the bedroom, a living room or a den where you want to unwind at the end of the day. However, they are ideal for children's rooms, or the hall, the stairway or the landing, or a bathroom where you want to discourage people from lingering too long. You will get the same effect with bold patterns in contrasting colors— bold geometrics in, say, black, orange and emerald on a white background or a floral pattern with pink, purple and green on a yellow

background will literally seem to jump out and hit you in the eye. Always bear these effects in mind when putting together a color scheme.

Contrasts of light and dark

The strongest contrast of all is black and white. These two true neutrals used together can have enormous impact—the black will absorb light whereas white reflects it back, giving the greatest possible visual difference. Give black and white schemes added interest with accents in warm or cold colors, depending on the atmosphere you want to create.

Modern colors

The strongest values of primary colors (red, blue and yellow) with secondary colors (orange, green and violet) are the boldest colors you can use, and combinations of these rainbow colors will create

Creating illusions

To make a large but not particularly tall room look more inviting, decorate the main surfaces—the walls and floor—to complement each other. Use window treatments that contrast with the walls to make the windows stand out more and look more important, as in the room on the right. You can apply the same technique with a drape above a bed, bath or sofa. You can break up a large area visually by using a bedcover or upholstery to contrast with the floor. Similarly, choose kitchen cabinets and worktops or bathroom furniture in colors that contrast strongly with the walls and floors. Link the scheme together with neutral tones on the woodwork, or as a background to a patterned fabric or wallcovering—but take care not to let these patterns look too tiny or too overpowering.

A SENSE OF SIZE
Contrasting color schemes will add interest to square, boring rooms and make large areas look less intimidating. In a

small space, a checkerboard floor, created by using contrasting-colored tiles, will look wider and, consequently, larger. Try black and white tiles, as in the room on the left, or navy blue and yellow, terra-cotta and cream, red and pale gray-green, and dark green and pink for good contrasting combinations. Paint the baseboards (and chair rail, if there is one) to match the lighter tile to increase the illusion further.

REDUCING THE HEIGHT
In the room on the left, red and white have been used to complement each other, in both the walls and the furniture, to break up a large wall area. In order to decrease the apparent height of a tall hall, bedroom or living room, paint the ceiling in a warm advancing color in a midtone; use the same color on the floor. Pick out cornices and baseboards in the same neutral, preferably white or pale cream; then use a cool, pale contrast on the walls.

To translate this into reality, a hall in a narrow multilevel house could be schemed in terra-cotta (for the ceiling and floor), white (for woodwork and ceiling moldings/covings), and pale sky blue for the main wall area. If there is a chair rail or picture rail, pick out the former in white and the latter in the terra-cotta to make the walls seem less tall. On the top left, a narrow, wedge-shaped room is made to look less tall and thin by having the wall split at the picture rail. The use of white above the rail and for the ceiling makes the ceiling itself seem bigger, which in turn makes the room appear less narrow.

To bring down a high bedroom ceiling, you could color it a clear blue and paint on a white cloudscape. For a more sophisticated effect, try a midnight blue ceiling scattered with gold stars.

SECONDARY COLORS ▼
The colors below lie opposite each other on the color wheel, but they are blended colors, created by mixing the three primary colors. A scheme where you highlight several shades of one color with touches of its complement will be interesting and stimulating.

COLOR OPPOSITES ▲
The colors above are opposite each other on the color wheel—all are shown in their strongest values with their complementary color opposite them. It is a good idea to lighten or darken one of the complementary pairs to create a comfortable room scheme.

SECONDARY COLORS ▼
The colors below are also complementary opposites, made by blending the primary colors but as a variation from those on the left. The strength of the colors has been varied to show the effective partnerships of deep blue with light tangerine and of dull green with rosy pink.

Color theory

CLEVER COLOR SCHEMES
The split complementary scheme is slightly more complex than a two-color complementary scheme. You select one main color, then combine it with the two colors that flank its complementary, or opposite, on the color wheel. This might give you red teamed with blue-green and yellow-green, orange with blue-green and blue-violet, or purple with red-orange and yellow-orange. For a stimulating but not overwhelming look, mix the values of the colors in such a scheme for a room that is comfortable as well as interesting.

ADJACENT COLORS
You can achieve contrasting schemes by using very different shades and tones of one color or of adjacent colors on the color wheel. If you use similar values of adjacent colors— strong blues and greens or soft pinks and apricots, for example—the result will be very unsettling and cold-looking in the first case, and dull and uninteresting in the second. To avoid this, mix the values to add interest and temper the effect with just a few accents in a color that complements them. Add touches of purple to a blue-green scheme and add depth to a peachy-pinky scheme with touches of green.

---

very bold, exciting schemes. Once you start to add white or black to any of these they become less striking, so use them in room schemes in a different way, by adding neutral black, white or shades of gray and cream to balance these strong hues. As a rule, these colors work best in modern settings. If you want to achieve a look of faded elegance in, say, a traditional living room or bedroom, use more subtle tones and paler values.

A light touch

One way of enhancing bold color schemes is by clever lighting. Make any item in the room stand out by focusing accent or display lighting on it, emphasizing the contrasts in its color or outline. Cornice lighting will focus attention on dramatic curtains, whereas uplights will make the ceiling look prominent. You can use light in the same way to define cornices or moldings that are in contrast to the surrounding colors.

Conversely, you can use soft, subtle lighting from wall lights and shielded pendants to throw a gentle glow, which will soften the effect of bold contrasts. Any even background light with no special focus will have this same muting effect on strong color schemes.

Contrasting textures

Introduce contrasts in texture in a room to add extra interest. Add some shiny, light-reflecting textures in the form of glazed chintz, satin, cotton sateen or moiré fabrics. Gloss paint on woodwork and satin finish paint or ceramic tiles on walls will also create a subtle sheen, as will mirrors, glass, polished wood or shiny metals.

Light-filtering textures that diffuse daylight can soften a bright, contrasting scheme, especially if you use them as window treatments. Lace, nets, muslins, coarsely woven sheers, slatted and rattan blinds, plantation shutters and cane screens will all help to make contrasts less dominant by dappling the light on them. Open-weave fabrics used as tablecovers, bedcovers or drapes; wicker, cane and rattan furniture; metal and trellis-work; feathery foliage—all will tone down strong contrasts, making them more comfortable.

Mauve and blue

Bright blue, deep mauve, white and various shades of green, set against each other, give this dining room a bright and stimulating atmosphere. There is a contrast, too, between the plain surfaces of the walls, the paintwork and the table, and the richly patterned plates and figures on the shelves and the tablecloth. This balance of detail and simplicity is vital in a room with such a strongly contrasting color scheme.

Yellow and red

The bright pinky red and daffodil yellow in this room need cooling with neutrals and with the broken texture of foliage. Neutral white on the woodwork and fresh green in the flowers and leaves have just the right effect. In an interesting contrast, very bright modern colors are given a traditional look by the damask patterns in the upholstery, the classic lines of the side table, the striped fabric of the pillows and the elegant accessories.

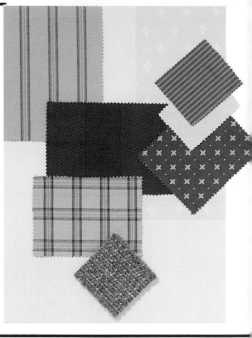

Maroon and blue

Two similarly dark, matte shades—deep blue and dull rusty maroon—combine to make a comfortable den/library, which looks warm and relaxing, just the place to browse and read. Brighter colors or a gloss finish might create an unsettling effect. The two strongly contrasting colors are drawn together in the curtains. The only other patterned detail is in the form of the decorative accessories.

Contrasting pottery

In a room where the paintwork has a matte finish, you can afford to jazz up the color scheme with accessories in shiny glass or with brightly glazed pottery, which reflect the light in an eye-catching way. Restrict yourself to picking up colors from the main scheme so that the effect is not too busy. Pastel colors would look entirely out of place in a rich, dark scheme, such as this one.

BOTH PICTURES: ROBERT HARDING PICTURE LIBRARY

Softening contrasts

The broken pattern of wicker furniture or the blended colors and reflected light from tinted glass can be used to make a very bright or contrasting scheme seem less bold.

BOTH PICTURES: ROBERT HARDING PICTURE LIBRARY

Effects of the light

If you want to create a cozy atmosphere in a room with rich contrasts, choose soft furnishings with a nonreflecting surface and avoid shiny damasks, leather, sateen or chintz.

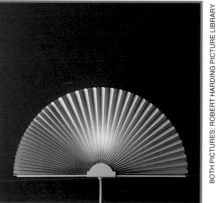

BOTH PICTURES: ROBERT HARDING PICTURE LIBRARY

Use uplights to draw attention to a painted ceiling or to reduce the feeling of height in a very tall room. This fan-shaped light gives a cozy glow, ideal for a comfortable and relaxing retreat.

Creating a mood WITH COLOR

Some rooms already have a mood and an atmosphere of their own; others are blank boxes, and it is up to you to give them ambience and character. More than anything, it is the way that you use color that determines the mood of a room.

ELIZABETH WHITING ASSOCIATES. INSET : THE PHOTOGRAPHERS LIBRARY

Welcoming

Fresh greens make a hall bright and welcoming. This simple color scheme uses tones of yellow-green. As with the woodland ferns, inset, the calm mood associated with green is warmed by the sunny yellow.

Warmth

In this bedroom, the darkness of the rich red walls gives a feeling of warmth, but the natural spicy tone also looks elegant and sophisticated. Print curtains and the patchwork bedspread lighten the mood, as does the neutral carpet. The overall feel is comfortable but traditional.

THE PHOTOGRAPHERS LIBRARY

ELIZABETH WHITING ASSOCIATES

Restful and cool

Blues, lilacs and white in a bedroom are calming; being cool, receding colors, they give an impression of spaciousness. Imagine going to sleep in the scented air and gentle mauves of a field of lavender.

Relaxed elegance

Where red or orange might be overstimulating, the pink and peachy tones made by adding white to either color are warm, comfortable and gentle on the eye. Just as the pinky blossom, above, needs a contrasting center of pink and green, the blue table-cover adds a vital accent to avoid the room feeling bland and dull.

Color theory

■ Bright yellows are stimulating and advancing, and reflect a lot of light, so you can use them in fairly large quantities (even in small spaces) without their being overpowering. Pale yellow will make a room look larger and lighter—ideal in a small bathroom that has mainly white fixtures.

■ Red is strongly advancing and can be overdominant, if you use strong values. It is also stimulating and dramatic, and will make a large room cozier; but it can make a small space seem uncomfortably claustrophobic, so use it with care. Red-orange and red-violet, used with red, create a discordant contrast, which can be very uncomfortable. Cool down strong reds with a receding color, such as green. But as these colors complement each other, they create a highly stimulating mood. For a more subtle effect, use candy pink with sage, burgundy with pale leaf green, or rose with forest green.

■ Green is the balance color, halfway between warm and cool on the color wheel, so it combines well with all the other colors. Create a vibrant mood with the warm colors, or a calming mood by mixing green with the cool colors.

With color you can create any atmosphere you want—from warm and welcoming to soothing and cool. Not surprisingly, color is the most important consideration in setting the tone of a room.

Characteristics of color

Each color has its own distinctive character and is traditionally associated with particular moods and feelings. Yellow is a joyful color—sunshine, spring flowers—the most outgoing color in the spectrum, symbolizing rebirth, life and creative energy. It is also associated with the mind, intellect and power. Paler yellows suggest spring, whereas the deeper mellow golds are associated with Mediterranean warmth and long sunny days or with the romantic glow of candlelight. Use yellow to bring warmth and sunlight into a dark, cold area, such as a basement or a room that is overshadowed by trees.

Yellow, partnered with blue and highlighted with white, will look fresh and clean, giving a Scandinavian look; red and yellow work well together, as long as there is enough tonal contrast (deep Indian red with subtle gold or mimosa yellow; deep rose with delicate lemon sorbet). Yellow and green create a country look, ideal for bringing a breath of air into a dark apartment. ▶

33

◀ Slightly dull blue gives a kitchen the impression of space, and because it does not reflect light strongly, it can tone down a room that gets a lot of sun. Blues are cooling, so accent them with warm colors, such as the red of the flowers or the bright refrigerator magnets.

▶ Cool down a warm, predominantly pink room, such as this bathroom, with green in the form of houseplants. This effect is ideal for summer; in winter, remove the greenery and replace it with autumn berries or leaves to give a cozier feeling.

Color theory

■ If you combine orange with green, the two colors act as a foil for each other and are a less-aggressive mix than red and green. Orange mixed with gray becomes terra-cotta, soft brick or chestnut brown—mellow autumn colors, which work well in large living areas and halls. Combine these colors with greens or blues to add depth to a sun-room.

Mustardy-golds and bronzes are rich and inviting, with a subdued warm glow, but greeny yellows can become cold. Some golden olives need clever lighting and color-matching—they look vibrant and rich in daylight, but cold and gray at night.

Shades of red

Red is the color of vitality, energy and excitement—even aggression. Red is also an appetite-inducing color (restaurants and food stores use it to persuade you to order more), so it is not always advisable for a dining room or a kitchen, if there are calorie counters in the family. Red can also make food look undercooked!

The subtler reds are more relaxing. Add white to make soft pinks—these are delicate and feminine, and associated with love and romance—an ideal color for a romantic bedroom or to warm up a cold bathroom. The grayed versions—plums, dusty rose, rich wines—are also easier to live with and add warmth with sophistication. Use these tones to lend style to an entry hall, create an intimate mood in a traditional dining room or make a large living area feel comfortable.

As red goes toward blue, it becomes lilac-pink or purple plum—sophisticated colors, which can add an air of mystery to a room, but beware, they can be a little cold and unwelcoming.

Blue with red can be very smart—navy with Indian red for a rich, intimate dining room or bedroom; pale sky blue with deep rose in a

ABODE LK

modern living room; mid-blue with primary red and a splash of yellow for a child's room. Use grays, creamy neutrals and white for a contrast to red and to give a scheme greater subtlety.

Orange combines the energy of red with the intellect of yellow. It is similar to yellow in that it is a sunny color and can bring warmth and sunlight to a dark or chilly area; but unlike yellow, it can be claustrophobic if you use strong values in a small space. It is better to add the warmth of orange to a room in the accents and accessories.

Orange lightened with white is more delicate, subtle and feminine. Soft peaches or apricots look good in traditional bedrooms and bathrooms, especially when highlighted with white, or contrasted with cream or gray to add warmth without being enclosing.

Natural greens

Green is nature's color, as shades such as grass, forest and leaf suggest. Its freshness adds sophistication to a large country living room or sparkle to sunless city space.

Some people are still superstitious about using green in decorating at all, because it is the alien color of snakes, frogs, crocodiles and even dragons! It is also associated with poison, which was traditionally stored in green bottles. In Victorian times, an arsenic-based pigment was used to create a bright green (used for dying fabrics and wallpapers), which resulted in some deaths before the cause was analyzed—this may be why green was regarded as unlucky!

Blue moods

Blue is the color of peace, harmony and devotion, ▶

◀ In a traditional bedroom, pale apricot looks soft and feminine. The natural wood of the bed and other furniture contributes to the feeling of gentle warmth, and the delicate white bed linen, frothy curtains and spriggy white daisies lend a feeling of lightness and prettiness. The overall mood is relaxing, peaceful and calm—a truly restful bedroom.

■ Add green accents in the form of plants. This has a cooling effect in summer, and you can remove them in winter when you want a cozier mood.

■ Blue is fairly low in reflective value and will also diffuse and soften bright sunlight, so use the gentler shades to tone down an overbright room or to add an oasis of calm to a sunny one.

■ Blue-green mixes—turquoise, peacock and jade—reflect more light than pure blue and are more lively. Use these to brighten up dark areas where you do not want to use yellowy colors.

■ The complementary colors for purple are jades, mint and lime green, and these mixes create fresh and stimulating schemes. Burnished yellows and deep golds will add richness and warmth to purple but can be quite distracting, so use with care.

■ Purple or violet lightened to make lavender, mauve or lilac can look as romantic as pink in a feminine bedroom, but look sophisticated if mixed with grape tones and subtle grays to create an elegant period living room.

■ Gray provides tonal balance and extra interest, but remember to add a few colored accents to bring a mainly gray scheme to life.

▶ Soft green mixed with blue and yellow at their brightest make a room scheme that is stimulating, warm and busy. Blue and green both recede, so alone can look very cold—the elements of yellow are essential for a sunny quality in the room.

and of blue horizons and gentle welcoming seas. The paler tones are often used to create an impression of endless space and a mood of calm relaxation. Blue often seems to be much colder than green, and gray-blues can appear dull and dirty, but you can spike them with white to give added life. Blue mixed with complementary terra-cotta, peach or coral will create a mood that is stimulating without being too disturbing, as long as there is enough contrast in tone.

Purple and violet are associated with royalty and are regal and dominating in their most vibrant tones. They will create an air of exotic mystery in a dark bedroom or a traditional dining room.

One-color schemes

Monochromatic schemes based on variations of one color give different effects according to what color you use. Warm colors will look inviting without being too enclosing, while cool colors will create a feeling of space and elegance.

◀ The opposite of a room with warm greens, shown above, this creamy white room, left, uses cool blue-greens as accents. The effect is an atmosphere that is cool and very calming. In the colder seasons, this room would need some bright highlights for warmth.

Color theory

■ True neutrals—black, white and gray—are not strictly colors, but can be used to create a link or contrast. (Creams, off-whites and "hint of" colors are accepted as neutrals, although all relate back to an original hue.) Schemes that are mainly neutral can be cold and boring—so introduce color in details to add interest but not distract the eye, in what is essentially a calm and relaxing color scheme.

CHAPTER 2

The Color Palette

Blue is the color which denotes harmony, loyalty and devotion; in heraldry, it symbolizes sincerity and piety. It is also associated with the Madonna; Medieval artists depicted her robes in blue to suggest heaven, chastity and faith. Blue in nature suggests infinity—stretches of sky and sea disappearing into the horizon, or the deep blue-black of space. The Greek sky gods, Jupiter, Juno and Mercury, were also traditionally symbolized by the color blue.

But blue has another side— "blue ruin" was once a name for bad gin, while "Blue Monday," the day before Shrove Tuesday, implied a day of alcoholic excess before Lent. And blue music, or the "blues," is associated with melancholy soul-searching.

Being a cool color, blue tends to create a calm, peaceful atmosphere, so is often chosen for schools and hospitals.

Bold contrasts

Blue looks striking mixed with strong, warm shades. Used with orange, its opposite or complementary on the color spectrum, it creates a vibrant scheme. Mix turquoise with burnt-orange, or Prussian blue with apricot, or navy with peach. Blue and yellow are a classic combination, bringing to mind summer, warmth and relaxation: the yellow of the sunshine, gold of sands and blue skies.

Remember, if you team strong, deep blues with bright reds, that the eye is dazzled if it focuses on primary red and blue together; bright blue letters set against a strong red ▶

Shoreline

Cool blue has a reflective quality, creating a light and spacious feel in this pretty living room. The golden browns of the wooden fireplace, shelves and furniture teamed with blue walls, echo the stretches of sand and mirrorlike pools of a low tide shoreline.

SHADES OF
BLUE

Add space and light to your home with versatile blue, and with it create a soothing, relaxed and peaceful atmosphere.

Color theory

■ Bold blues, such as turquoise or peacock, have high reflective values and, therefore, brighten up dark areas. Used at each end of a long, narrow room, with a paler value of the color in between, it will make the room seem much wider. And for rooms that are not very wide but have high ceilings, such as a hall, paint the ceiling a deep, rich sapphire or Madonna blue. Highlight cornice or coving and ceiling moldings in white to contrast and define.

■ As blue is a cold color, it will create an impression of space and airiness but it can also be chilly, so look at your room—its size, shape and orientation (which direction it faces) and the amount of natural daylight it receives, before reaching a decision. Take all this, as well as the architectural style, into consideration when planning a scheme, before deciding on the amount of blue to use and the depth of the color.

■ Kitchens are often decorated in cool colors because they are the scene of lots of hot, steamy cooking activity. However, once the stove is switched off, the temperature can plummet. If you choose blue for your kitchen, combine it with pine cabinets for warmth.

Stormy seas

The blues and grays of a stormy sea provide the inspiration for this hallway scheme—used together, they give a look of understated elegance. A pretty blue leaded-glass window creates a focal point, while white woodwork and black and white tiles balance the gray tones.

Blue skies

The classic combination of bright blue and white gives this bathroom a crisp, fresh appeal, reminiscent of a blue summer sky complete with cottony clouds. Willow-pattern plates and delft plates on the wall continue the traditional theme, along with blue and white wall tiles. The silver statue adds a striking finishing touch.

ARCAID · SIMON KENNY

ROBERT HARDING PICTURE LIBRARY

◀ Blue is perfect for a light sun porch or a glass-walled living room, as it echoes the color of the sky and provides a visual link with the blues and greens of the outdoors. Rich shades of plum add a touch of warmth.

▶ Pale blues and yellows create a calm, restful atmosphere—ideal for a child's bedroom or nursery. Accessories in neutral shades—wood, cream and beige—or splashes of bright blue work well with this combination.

background are almost impossible to read. Many children like the stimulation of a bright blue and red nursery or playroom, but such a scheme will need a neutral, such as off-white, beige or shades of pale brown, for balance.

Countryside colors

Blue and green used together bring to mind the colors of the countryside—grass, trees and fields underneath a blue sky. They also create a comfortable, relaxed ambience, as they are "neighborly" colors, next to each other on the color spectrum. These countryside colors were popular with William Morris and the Arts and Crafts Movement in the latter half of the 19th century. To add warmth to blue and green schemes, they used natural beige, golds or deep Indian red, together with light, limed and bleached oaks.

Used in a sun porch, blue echoes the sky and, combined with the green of the plants, provides a visual link with the outdoors. In the summer, the effect is cool and refreshing, and in winter, bright rugs or natural floorcoverings add a touch of warmth.

ROBERT HARDING PICTURE LIBRARY

ROBERT HARDING PICTURE LIBRARY

▲ A powerful powder-blue bathroom scheme—in walls, woodwork and furniture—receives a dramatic lift with a horizontal striped border of white, blue and green.

▶ Turquoise color-washed walls echo shades of the sea in this bathroom scheme. White accessories and a large mirror add freshness and create a sense of space.

▲ Add warmth to cool shades of gray-blue with rich terra-cotta. Here, a gray-blue carpet and curtains are teamed with warm terra-cotta walls to create the perfect backdrop for the focal point of the room: a colorful patterned sofa in the same shades.

▲ For a striking color scheme, use bright blue with accents in vibrant shades of orange-red. Here, a gilt-framed mirror and pictures add a touch of opulence.

Natural shades

Golden shades of pine are perfect for adding warmth to a blue living room and for creating a country look. Curtains and carpets are kept plain, in neutral shades of off-white and brown. The alcove shelves and mantelpiece provide plenty of space for a varied selection of ornaments, a focal point of the room—crockery, dried flowers, jugs and even an abacus.

Warm natural wood complements shades of pale blue and bright blue.

Cool gray-blues

Cool steel-blue and pale shades of gray to white work together to create a simple but sophisticated scheme for this hallway. The look is minimalist: Softly sponged subtle gray and white walls are left uncluttered, with only two small monochrome pictures and plain vases as accessories. Black and white floor tiles are a traditional way of enhancing the feeling of space in a small room.

Gray-blue, with subtle shades of pale gray, black and white, creates an elegant look.

Classic colors

Blue with white is a traditional color scheme: The Victorians collected blue-and-white crockery, and soft blue and white was a popular Georgian combination. Here, the silver statue, with gold fixtures on the tub and the ceramic basin, add a touch of opulence. The painted black floor provides a stark contrast to the blue and white, while cream tiles and a wooden washstand with pink and white accessories soften the overall look.

Splashes of pink and accessories in wood soften a bright blue-and-white scheme.

Country look

For a country theme based around shades of pale blue, choose plain wooden furniture, with neutral colors for curtains and carpets—add interest with bright accents and a collection of accessories. Arts and Crafts-style furniture, with its plain lines in solid wood, works well. Tapestry pillows in bright blue are perfect on a backdrop of calico or off-white, and a patterned rug in rich terra-cottas and earth tones brightens up a neutral brown carpet. There's endless range when it comes to accessories—earthenware jugs, terra-cotta pots, bright blue and white vases, and bowls with dried flowers in subtle shades all complement a pale blue background.

ARCAID – KEN KIRKWOOD

CAMERA PRESS LTD – TREVOR RICHARDS

Minimalist styling

Just a few, carefully chosen accessories are all you need to enhance an elegant, understated gray and blue scheme. For example, a single mirror with an unusual frame can act as a focal point, and if strategically placed, add light and depth to a narrow hallway. For furniture, choose unusual pieces, such as this wrought-iron chair, that rely on shape and form rather than color or decoration. Keep the lines of the furniture uncluttered; you don't need any pillows or throws. For smaller accessories, choose plain items, such as a few wooden boxes placed on a windowsill or a small table. If you opt for pictures or photographs, don't use too many; again, one or two carefully chosen, unusual items are better than a vast array, which would look cluttered.

THE IRON DESIGN COMPANY

Eclectic accessories

THE PHOTOGRAPHERS' LIBRARY

Traditional blue and white is an ideal backdrop for accessories in natural neutral shades or for striking opulent decorations in gold, silver or brass. Both add warmth to what is basically a cool scheme. You don't have to opt for one style or the other—mix wooden picture frames, towel rails, wicker chairs and baskets with either Art Deco- or Art Nouveau-style statues, pewter vases or pretty silver and glass perfume bottles. Add splashes of bright, contrasting color—candles in warm shades of dark pink or yellow, arranged along a washstand or shelf, are ideal.

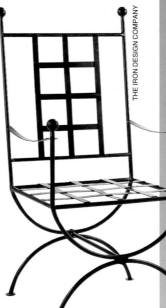

ELIZABETH WHITING ASSOCIATES; INSET - THE PHOTOGRAPHERS' LIBRARY

SHADES OF
Green

Explore the endless variety **the color green offers—from** cool and relaxing **schemes to** warm, vibrant contrasts.

Green is the color of nature—we associate it with flowers and foliage, fields, forests and rivers. It suggests hope and regeneration, as the green springtime shoots push their heads above the barren earth after the long, hard winter. In heraldry, green is also the symbol of growth and hope; it is the sacred color of Islam, too. For the Christian Church, green vestments symbolize the hope of the resurrection and eternal life, while in Medieval times, green was the color of the Holy Trinity.

The color green may evoke spiritual and positive elements, but it does have a more sinister side, too. Bright green, ridged bottles were used to indicate that the substance inside was poisonous (the ridges were for the blind or those with poor vision). And an arsenic-based pigment, in a virulent shade of green known as "Paris Green," was used in some Victorian wallpapers and paints, resulting in the deaths of decorators and craftsmen. This might account for the color green having unlucky connotations at one time.

As most greens are restful and receding, they create a calm impression of space in a room; they are ideal for sunless rooms or dark basements. Green also provides a visual link with the garden in living rooms, dining rooms and sun porches. And because it is a cool color, it works well in kitchens, which are often hot, steamy areas of activity!

Bold green schemes

From lime to shades of aqua, green comes in infinite varieties. Made up of blue and yellow, green is often known as the balance color, as it can appear both cool (blue-green) and warm (yellow-green). This means it works just as well combined with bright, warm colors or cool, dark shades.

As green is the complement of red (its opposite color), together the two colors create a vibrant look, especially if strong tones of both are used. Remember, red is the advancing color and green the receding color, so the former will always seem dominant. For a balanced scheme with equal amounts of warm and cool shades, you need to use about one-third red and two-thirds green.

There may be a saying that "blue and green should never be seen," but this combination can be effective in interior decoration, especially if there is sufficient contrast in tone. ▶

Restful shades

For a restful, welcoming country-style look, team yellow-green with neutral shades. Here, the green ceiling combines with the warm tones of antique pine to echo the look of fresh pistachios and their shells. The neutral off-white walls complement the green perfectly, while a richly patterned rug in earth tones completes the look.

Cool and sophisticated

Deep forest green wallpaper and mahogany give a sophisticated air to this classic dining room. In the 18th and 19th centuries, dark green was a popular color for walls, ideal for setting off oil paintings in ornate gold frames. Here, the claret lamp shade and chair seats provide a rich contrast, while the white ceiling lifts the look.

Spring flowers

Green complements any floral theme, as it brings to mind the color of fresh foliage. In this elegant bedroom scheme, herb green and white are used with a floral wallpaper—peach flowers on a crisp pale blue background—to create a fresh, springlike look. The flowers on the headboard and the bedspread continue the theme.

Color theory

■ Green livens up a scheme mainly based on creamy-beige natural neutrals: Green paintwork, walls and ceiling, or green incorporated in a patterned fabric will add an extra dimension to natural woods, brick, jutes and hessians, seagrass, coir and rush matting.

■ For an elegant, sophisticated look, combine green with a gray, black and white neutral scheme. Add warm accents in shades of red or orange to prevent the ambience from becoming cold and unwelcoming.

■ Blues, purples and lilacs are next to green on the cool side of the color wheel, and used together these colors can help create an impression of space. Combine the darker greens with pale blues, soft lilacs, and lavenders with a touch of purple. If the effect is too cool, add strong magenta pink. This scheme works well in west-facing bedrooms, south-facing living rooms with a country feel, and traditional bathrooms .

■ Green and terra-cotta, peach or orange have a natural harmony, and they are often found together in nature—the colors of early autumn, for example. Used in a decorating scheme, these combinations create a calm, relaxed atmosphere.

▼ In this striking bedroom scheme, vibrant forest green provides a bold contrast with subtler shades of aqua. Neutral colors—here, a plain wooden floor and dark wood chest of drawers and table—work with pale shades of green to create a calm, relaxed atmosphere. They are also an ideal backdrop for the splashes of vibrant green, which could become overwhelming if used with other bright colors or over a large area. The pretty, dusky pink rose border at the top of the wall, and the patchwork quilt in shades of pale yellow, blue and brown add the finishing touch.

Combine pale sky and turquoise blues with deep foliage green for elegance, strong lime with navy blue for a striking effect, pale minty greens with lilac-blues for a refreshing look. Or you can use a mid-, powder blue with olive for a sophisticated scheme. But as most of these combinations are cool, add warmth with contrasting accents in pinks, pale peach, terra-cotta, ochers and golds, bold scarlet or plum tones. Bring them into the scheme in fabrics and borders or as accessories.

Lighting green

Dark greens, particularly the yellow-olive tones, tend to absorb light—under artificial lighting they retain the yellow, which appears to alter the surface color so it looks darker and duller. Dark green flooring, upholstery, curtains or wallcoverings can appear totally different at night, taking on a grayish cast. If you have matched a scheme in natural daylight, you could be surprised when the lamps are lit at night! Always look at color samples at home, under the artificial light in which they will be seen.

If you are using green, avoid bulbs with a yellowish cast; silvered spots or a silver reflector will improve the colors. Highlight dark green items, using cornice lighting for window treatments or uplights to enhance green ceilings. If you add greenery to a scheme with plants, these look wonderful back-lit, giving foliage a magical quality and throwing interesting shadows on walls and ceilings.

▲ Chalky pastel shades of pale mint green and powder blue, painted directly on the rough plaster, are the focal point in this country-style bedroom. The key to this look is rustic simplicity; accessories—a small patterned rug, a patchwork quilt and an unframed picture—are kept to a minimum, with bare wooden floors and plain furniture. Soft greens used with cool, pale colors create a light, spacious look.

▲ Create impact with vivid green accessories, used here with deep blue. The rich yellow-green sofa is covered with dark blue pillows, and the midnight-blue rug has a bright green border. Bright green and dark blue vases and bowls on the coffee table complete the look. The warm, pale creamy yellow walls, combined with natural materials—terra-cottas, wood and wicker—complement bold blue and green accessories.

◄ Green is an ideal color for any bathroom, evoking images of water—sea-green or aqua—from the palest to deepest shades. Here, a light sea-green contrasts with white tiles to create a clean, crisp look. The chest of drawers coordinates with the dark-wood framed prints adorning every wall, while the pretty pink and green rug, and glass and silver accessories soften the overall look.

◄ Pale green combined with gold creates an air of sophistication in this living room. Gold accessories—the gilt-framed mirror, picture frames and gold ornaments on the mantel—add a luxurious, warm touch to the backdrop of cool, pale green walls. The bright yellow coving, gold-spattered picture rail and chest, and the piping on the sofa continue the theme.

ABODE UK

47

Calm naturals

ABODE UK

Soft greens combined with neutral colors, such as off-white and pale browns, create a calm, restful look. Natural materials—antique pine, terracotta, wicker—provide the ideal complement for green, echoing muted woodland colors. Splashes of bright green foliage, from trailing plants to large ornamental palms or bamboo, add a vibrant contrast.

Combine soft shades of green with natural wood colors for a calm, restful look.

PHOTOGRAPHY BY LIZZIE ORME

Shades of luxury

ROBERT HARDING PICTURE LIBRARY – JAN BALDWIN

Sumptuous, deep shades of dark green are set off perfectly by accessories in rich wine colors. During Queen Victoria's reign, the popular Scottish Baronial style combined deep reds and greens with tartans and the rich browns of solid mahogany furniture. Dark greens need careful lighting—here, a crisp white ceiling and a large window with a floral curtain maximize the available natural light.

Shades of green used with contrasting colors of red and plum create a vibrant scheme.

Fresh florals

ROBERT HARDING PICTURE LIBRARY

For a pretty bedroom scheme that brings a breath of fresh spring air into your home, combine plain, herb or leaf greens with floral designs on crisp white or pale backgrounds; a dark background could make the room seem closed in. Choose delicate designs in shades of dusky pink, sunshine yellow, peach or apricot—these colors will add a touch of warmth to cool shades of soft, pale green and off-white tints.

Herb and leaf greens complement perfectly the warm tones of spring flowers.

Woodland tones

Pottery housed in a cupboard, in a display cabinet or even on a plain display shelf provides a simple but effective way of accessorizing a soft green living room. Choose tones in mint, aqua and olive green to complement the decor or opt instead for a complete contrast with splashes of bright yellow and orange. Use plants in a wooden bowl and even fresh fruit in a plain glass bowl to continue the natural theme.

Color theory

■ Green has long been thought of as a calm and relaxing color. At one time, it was thought to provide relief for tired eyes: Actors rested in "the green room" in a theater, which was painted a pale green, to give their eyes a rest from the glare of the footlights. And awnings were often made of green fabric to filter out harsh sunlight.

Vibrant colors

Striking decorating schemes that use rich dark greens need accessories in strong, vibrant colors for a balanced look. Bright scarlets or plums work well with green: In the dining room, mix a scarlet tablecloth with forest green napkins. As bright red teamed with deep green is a traditional festive look, a decorative variation of this table setting with a centerpiece is ideal for Christmas. Continue the red and green theme, using glassware with colorful motifs or elegant red or green china. Create a warm, cozy atmosphere with strategically placed bright red candles or lamps with red shades.

Color theory

■ Bright red and dark forest green are complementary colors, as they fall opposite each other on the color wheel. Used together they create a vibrant, stimulating scheme. As red is the warmer color, it will tend to stand out, or advance, more than the cool dark green, which will recede.

Pretty accessories

Pretty, elegant accessories—glass perfume bottles with silver lids or silver-backed hairbrushes and mirrors—are perfect for a floral bedroom. Choose delicate fabrics, such as lace and silk, for curtains, throws and pillow covers; use soft tones of ivory, pale blue, pink or plain, crisp white. Echo the design on fabrics and wallcoverings with fresh flowers in delicate shades of pink, arranged in a plain white china vase or a glass vase. Use simple painted wooden furniture in green or white with stenciled flower motifs to contrast with the floral theme.

Color theory

■ A color scheme of soft greens and white, with warm accents in dusky pink, peach or subtle red, creates a light and airy feel and is ideal for a bedroom, a living room or a hallway. Add warm accents in the form of floral motifs on wallcoverings and furnishing fabrics to create a traditional chintzy country style.

Summer colors

Yellow, especially combined with blue, is the true color of summer—June skies, sunshine, sand and summer flowers. These are an ideal contrasting combination to bring brightness to an east-facing cottage kitchen or living room.

THE PHOTOGRAPHERS LIBRARY

ABODE UK

SHADES OF
Yellow

Yellow is one of the easiest colors to use in decorating—it brings a touch of sunshine, warmth, space and light into your home.

Yellow is the color of well-being and of the intellect—associated with the mind, creative energy (derived from the sun's life-giving rays) and power. It also symbolizes wealth—the color of pure gold, money, gleaming brass, gilt and jewelry. In Medieval times, yellow was added to manuscripts and paintings to suggest royalty, privilege and pageantry; and in heraldry, yellow symbolizes

Color theory

■ Combine yellow with warm, cool or neutral colors to create many different effects and interior styles. Yellow has been used successfully over the centuries to improve many a humble home and enhance more opulent houses and castles.

■ When yellow and golds are mixed with the cooler colors of the spectrum, the effect will be bright and stimulating. Yellow with glossy leaf and dark greens suggests nature—foliage and flowers—which creates a crisp, fresh mood for a living room or a sun porch.

■ Yellow with lilac, violet or purple will create a stimulating scheme, as they are true complementary, or opposite, colors. Vary the tones for a more subtle look: rich gold and brass with lilac or lavender, bluish-purple with pale primrose, plum or wine with lemon. Combine yellow with vivid turquoise, peacock or lapis lazuli blues and strong jade greens to give a scheme that has a Mediterranean flavor.

■ Subtle, deep gold with turquoise, midnight or Madonna blue is a Medieval color scheme (as seen in illuminated manu-scripts and paintings). This combination will set a rich, traditional style, which works well in large foyers.

Fresh flowers

Yellow with green accents brings a flowery look to a room. Here, a creamy background to the wallpaper provides a gentle foil to the brighter bed linen for a restful bedroom.

Soft tones

Faded values—washed denim blues and blue-grays with creamy floral whites, sorbet yellow and scuffed golden tans—suggest an 18th-century Gustavian style popular in Scandinavian countries and used to good effect in this elegant and peaceful living room.

honor and loyalty.

In nature, yellow is the color of spring flowers: pale primrose, creamy narcissus yellow, glowing crocus gold and the "shout-for-joy" yellow of daffodils. All these tones will warm up a cold bedroom or a clinical bathroom, and will bring a touch of sunshine into a room with little or no natural light.

Autumn yellow becomes the colors of the harvest, which will add richness and elegance to a dark living room and a warm, intimate atmosphere to a formal dining room.

Yellow schemes

Yellow can also be used on its own with a neutral, and because it is such a warm, inviting color, it works well with whites, grays, browns, beiges and black. Or try a monochromatic effect: yellow with yellow for a tone-on-tone scheme, which will create a sunshine effect. Remember to vary the strengths of the color to create plenty of visual interest.

Single color schemes need a little color contrast to be truly effective, so add accents in a cool color, such as green or blue, as part of upholstery fabric that combines all the other colors in the rest of the scheme. The blue or green could be echoed ▶

▲ **Many woods used for furniture and fixtures are yellow or golden in tone, and will add a mellow and warming look to a scheme using neighboring colors of soft cream, yellow and olive green.**

again in some of the accessories, depending on the use of the room.

If you are nervous about using very bright, strong yellows in a room, golden-toned natural neutrals will introduce the color and its warm sunny appeal without being overpowering. Or you can use stronger yellows discreetly—as part of a multicolored pattern on fabric, floor or wallcovering, or in the form of accents, which are easy and often inexpensive to change.

Seasonal touches

Try adding some strong daffodil yellow and deep bronze golds to a scheme in the autumn and winter, and replacing them with paler creamy whites or cooler golden-greens in the spring and summer.

If your newly decorated room looks bathed in warm sunlight, add some sharp color contrasts in accents to emphasize the effect. Bold blues, jades, lilacs, rich greens, deep terra-cottas, stark black and sparkling white all combine well with yellow. Once you have a touch of this exciting, uplifting color in a room, you will want to introduce more and more into your color schemes.

◀ **Yellow, used with accents of Indian red, deep terra-cotta or wine, will look bold and exciting but will need offsetting with a cool, clear neutral. Here, the soft creamy upholstery and plain ivory ceiling add the necessary cooling influence.**

▶ **If you use yellow on a light-reflecting surface—chintz, silk fabrics, laminates, gloss or satin-finish paint or ceramic tiles, as in this bathroom—bear in mind that the color will seem stronger than when it is used on a light-diffusing surface.**

◄ Rooms schemed in yellow can look very different, depending on the shade you use. The daffodil and white stripe in the bathroom gives a much gentler color than the orangey yellow of the adjacent rooms.

► Napoleon loved yellow, gold, brass, gilt and black. This sophisticated living room with its mainly yellow theme is accented with dark furniture and elegant drapes to emulate a classic Empire look.

▲ Yellow will maximize any natural daylight or sunshine and reflect it, so it is an ideal color to select to give a warm, welcoming look to a really dark corner or area, such as a hall or a stairway.

Sunshine colors

ABODE UK

Even in a well coordinated scheme, such as this combination of bright yellow and deep, lapis lazuli blue, where all the accessories match, it is important to add color accents to prevent the look from becoming monotonous. The white of the table lamp and the pinky tones of the bunch of flowers adds just the right touch of nonprimary interest to the color scheme.

Combine primary colors and add nonprimary accents to create a bold, stimulating scheme.

PHOTOGRAPHY BY LIZZIE ORME

Faded elegance

ROBERT HARDING PICTURE LIBRARY – HENRY BOURNE

Muted colors, such as the soft yellows and faded blue-gray of this living room, create a restful atmosphere. But muted colors require contrasts of tone, which are provided by the polished wood of the table lamps and the dark gray-green of the coffee table and the foliage. Plants offer an ideal opportunity to adjust the look of your color scheme without recourse to actual decorating!

Several tones of yellow with blue-gray accents create a classic Gustavian scheme.

Spriggy florals

ROBERT HARDING PICTURE LIBRARY

If you are going to use boldly patterned fabrics, make sure that you set them against a background of much plainer, less bright colors so as to avoid a disturbing scheme of battling patterns. The small sprigs of the curtain fabric and wallpaper are very light and create a feeling of texture rather than of pattern. In a scheme of adjacent yellows and greens, wood is a perfect foil for accessories and details.

Use a palette of sunny yellow, leaf green and light wood for a soft, natural look.

Sun and sky

In a kitchen/dining room, the range for using richly colored accessories is unlimited. Extend your chosen color scheme with table linen or upholstery, as on the left and at bottom left, or with a collection of decorative glassware, wicker or kitchenware, as shown on the left and below. Even if you adhere to the same tones of the same colors, introduce variations of texture with light-reflecting materials, such as glass and matte painted wicker.

A boldly patterned fabric, such as the one used to cover the seat of the chair, left, makes a very effective accent. But beware of using these highly contrasting designs for larger areas, as they can easily become overpowering.

Color theory

■ To the Ancient Greeks, yellow represented fire and sun, the arts and learning; it was the color of Athena, the goddess of wisdom. For Christians and Hindus, yellow symbolizes life and truth; saffron robes worn by Buddhist monks are a sign of humility. To the Chinese, yellow represents the color of the earth.

Pottery and porcelain

No one can expect to have a different set of china to match each room in which it might be used. The modern, abstract designs on the tea set, below, are very different in style from the Empire-style wreath designs of the living room. However, the porcelain echoes some of the colors of the room and has the same, muted tones. A flower vase in a softly distressed blue matches the tones of the room perfectly. Select flowers to match or to complement your overall scheme; they are an easily changed accessory that make all the difference to the appearance of a room.

Color theory

■ Yellow is associated with food and flavor: spices, such as saffron, turmeric and mace, the hot tones of mustard and exotic Oriental and Asian foods. Yellow peppers, golden squash and sweet corn are synonymous with Mediterranean cooking and can give a decorative scheme the same warm feeling.

Yellow with wood and neutrals

A mainly yellow scheme with a background of soft cream is a perfect setting for mellow wood furniture, such as the washstand, left. Even dark-stained wood will look comfortable if it has a soft, polished finish so that it reflects the light. In sharp contrast, choose crisp white linen sheets and pillowcases—they are wonderfully fresh to the touch and, being plain, provide a cool expanse of a neutral color. A gentle yellowy sconce, below, adds a finishing touch.

Color theory

■ Yellow reflects light, so it will look brighter spread over a large area or hung at a big window than you might suppose from a small sample! Try to see as large a piece of fabric, wallcovering, flooring or paint sample as possible in the room where it will be used and in day and night lighting to make sure you don't overdo it.

Firing the appetite

Red is an appetite-inducing color—often used in fast food outlets to encourage larger orders! More subtle values of red, however, are often used by restaurants to persuade the customers to linger over a meal—it makes a comfortable atmosphere for indulgent dining.

SHADES OF RED

Associated with energy, joy, aggression, warmth and even danger, red is a challenging color to use in decorative schemes.

Red is the most exciting color in the spectrum—the color of danger and fire, blood and revolution—and the most attention-grabbing color of all, used for stop lights, warning signs and fire engines.

Red has been seen differently by various cultures throughout history. To the Chinese, it represented luck and happiness, and in recent times, revolution and discipline. To American Indians, it symbolized the desert and disaster; in Ancient Egypt, it was the color of the sun god, Ra; while in Greek and Roman mythology, it was associated with the gods of the harvest. It is also the color of lust—hence the terms "red-light district" and "scarlet woman"—although traditionally brides in Japan wear this variously interpreted color.

Decorating with red

Red is the hottest of the warm, advancing colors on the color wheel, and its adjacent colors—red-orange and red-violet—are also hot. When these adjacent colors are used with red, they can create an uncomfortable contrast, so think twice before ▶

Decorating tricks

Make an unwelcoming room seem warmer with cherry red. In this room, red walls and a red-reflecting gold ceiling create a cozy atmosphere, as the two seem closer together. Coving and the fireplace, in cream, add the necessary definition and lighten the overall effect.

Reflected colors

Red in a bathroom scheme will reflect on your skin, giving you a rosier image in the mirror, so beware of false impressions. However, red is essentially a warm color, so it works well in a spacious bathroom, with strongly contrasting blue in the shower tiles adding the necessary touch of sparkling cool, receding color.

Color theory

■ Red can be a subtle and delicate color when diluted with white to become pink, which is associated with femininity. But it also symbolizes good health and high spirits; if you are "in the pink," you are looking well; if you see the world through "rose-colored glasses," then you are optimistic and "everything's rosy"! Pink is associated with love, romance and sophistication; and when blue is added to create lilac or mauve, the color takes on an aura of mystery.

■ The more subdued versions of red are easier to live with in terms of decoration—use these to warm up a cold bathroom without losing the sense of space and light; use deep rose and wine to add elegance to a formal dining room or country-style living room.

■ Red is a warm, advancing color, which can make a large, cold space seem smaller, warmer and more welcoming. But red can also be enclosing and claustrophobic or over-stimulating if you use bright values indiscriminately. More subtle values—pink, rose, wine, brick or burgundy—will be inviting without making a space seem smaller.

using them as the basis of any room scheme.

Avoid quantities of strong red in kitchens—especially for the diet-conscious, as it is an appetite enhancer. It can also make meat look undercooked, which can be deceptive! For a cozy kitchen scheme, try sunny yellow with subtle Indian red.

In a long, narrow room, use red in a fairly strong (but not too vivid) value on the narrow end walls, or for a floor-to-ceiling and wall-to-wall window treatment if one end of the room is glazed. Use a contrasting color, such as a neutral or cool gray or green, for the longer walls. It helps to have a bold floor treatment: two contrasting colors or tones in tiles, laid checkerboard fashion, or in crossways stripes will create an illusion of greater width.

Color combinations

Combine strong wine red with minty green, or Indian red with lime green to warm up a cold kitchen; some of the midtone greens, spiced up with glowing sunset red, can also be effective and will refresh a wintertime sun-room.

Red with purple or violet is synonymous with royalty and richness, but this is a very dominant combination, especially in the stronger values. Use deeper values of blue-purple with wine or Indian red (especially in tartan check fabric) to create a Scottish baronial theme.

Forget the rules!

Red decor is said to be stimulating and exciting, while green is considered to be the opposite; yet experiments have been carried out using different values of red, including pink, on cell walls for violent prisoners, with calming results. So forget the rules and use reds just the way you want, with flair and imagination!

ABODE UK

SANDERSON

FIRED EARTH

▲ Light-absorbing surfaces (the flat red walls) and light-filtering textures (the latticed windows, fringed curtains and twiggy giant hogweed) reduce the strength of the dominant red of this room, creating an atmosphere that is warmly welcoming and comfortable on the eye.

▲ Red is rarely used as a monochromatic scheme, unless in very subtle values of pink and deep rose/wine. If you want to use red as the only color, combine it with true neutrals—black, white and gray—for a crisp, modern feel. For a more subtle effect, combine a deeper tone of red, as above, with accepted neutrals—creams, off-whites, beiges and natural wood colors—and with matte, neutral tiles as a floorcovering.

◀ A room scheme with a great deal of red can be successful if the main color is muted and softened and if it is not made stronger with reflective, shiny surfaces. More akin to rusty brown than red, the dominant color in this spacious bedroom creates an atmosphere that is warm without being overpowering.

ROBERT HARDING PICTURE LIBRARY – BRIAN HARRISON

▲ Before the mid-19th century, red pigments were expensive and rare; but in Victorian times, they became cheaper, and red flock wallpapers, imitating 18th-century damasks, were popular as a foil for hanging paintings.

▶ Although they can be disturbing together, red and green can also be very restful and comfortable. Dulled shades of both colors, lightened by cream in the walls and rug, give of touch of baronial elegance.

◀ In the late 18th century, Oriental reds became popular, and many a room was decorated around glossily lacquered red cabinets or Persian and Turkish carpets. Later, in the Victorian era, deeper Indian red (with more than a hint of terra-cotta in its makeup), as shown here, was used as a foil for Oriental and Asian artifacts. Red has always been suggestive of wealth and opulence and, in its more sophisticated tones, represents the epitome of taste and elegance in decorative schemes.

THE PHOTOGRAPHERS LIBRARY

59

Period elegance

Strong, deep reds used with creamy yellow, deep golds, gilt and brass create a very 18th-century, Regency look. This is an ideal scheme to use for a period flavor in a formal dining room— especially with the introduction of shiny black in the lamp shades and with the sparkling elegance of the chandelier and ruched fabric ceiling.

Shiny polished wood is a natural complement to rich tones of red and gentle neutral cream.

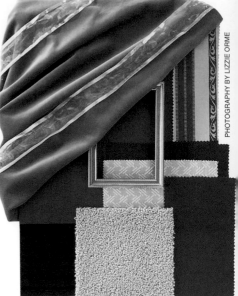

Touches of gold

This living room makes a definite style statement; it is a room for a flamboyant, extroverted personality. The shiny quality of the red, both on the walls and upholstery, is increased by gold sponging and embroidery. Vital contrasts, in the form of the cream mantel and cornice, lighten the room; the soft marbled baseboard and rug absorb some of the dazzle and shine.

Red, gold and cream are an opulent and strongly contrasting combination.

Bold contrasts

Although green is the true complement to red, blue can create a similar impact; In fact, red and blue together can seem to cancel each other out or simply look very dazzling. Normally plenty of tonal contrast will prevent this, but in a room where two strong values are used together, the light-filtering blinds, quarry tile flooring, dull metal washstand and gnarled basket and stand add vital contrasts in texture.

Use primary colors together with care for a warm and stimulating atmosphere.

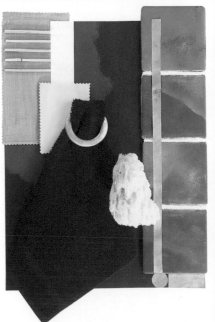

Classic style

A classically elegant dining room setting such as this demands rich and traditional accessories and furniture. Choose polished wood furniture with a deep shine and brass trimmings, and light up a sideboard laden with sparkling crystal and cutlery with small, atmospheric lights, such as the candelabra-style lamp, below right. Flowers are never out of place on a dining table, and this warm red room and traditional formal setting call for crimson roses. Modern accessories would be distinctly out of place here—a few suitable accessories are far more in keeping than a whole collection of items that are too modern.

ROBERT HARDING PICTURE LIBRARY

BCTH PICTURES: ELIZABETH WHITING ASSOCIATES

Color theory

■ Red is the hottest color and the nearest in wavelength to infrared, which actually produces a sensation of heat. Temper the energy of a mainly red room by breaking up the impact of all-red walls with paintings and by drawing the eye with contrasting drapes. Cleverly handled, red can create striking and successful schemes.

A riot of red

ELIZABETH WHITING ASSOCIATES

Making a definitive decorating statement in red takes confidence and panache. Choose a profusion of shiny pillows in light-reflecting damasks and add unusual and eye-catching accessories, such as the set of Russian dolls, below. Floor treatments need to be more practical—a multicolored patterned rug will absorb a lot of wear and tear and still look good.

ROBERT HARDING PICTURE LIBRARY; INSET: THE PHOTOGRAPHERS L BRARY

Color theory

■ Surface textures can alter how we see color: Shiny, light-reflecting materials (gloss paint, ceramic tiles, silk, glazed chintz) bounce light back at you, making the color look brighter than it really is. Light-absorbing textures seem to swallow the color because they absorb a lot of light.

Clean colors

This bathroom succeeds in being simple and bright without looking clinical. Choose towels and other fabric items in colors that match or tone with the main theme of red and blue and add accents in a bold contrasting color, such as yellow, for the faucets. The feeling is modern and bright, so fresh blue glassware is a perfect accessory, adding freshness and light with its reflecting surface. In a bold scheme such as this, when in doubt opt for shades of the main colors to avoid a look that is too hectic or busy.

THE PHOTOGRAPHERS LIBRARY

RHPL – TREVOR RICHARDS

ROBERT HARDING PICTURE LIBRARY – LUCINDA SYMONS

Color theory

■ Red is directly opposite green on a color wheel, so if you stare at a bright red object for a few seconds, then look away, you will see a green after-image. Bright reds will look stimulating, even disturbing, with greens, so confine such combinations to rooms where you do not want the family to linger, such as the only bathroom!

SHADES OF
Pink

From the palest pastel shades and sweet ice-cream tones to brightest cerise and tulip, pink is one of the most versatile and easy to use colors in decorating.

Pink symbolizes good health and high spirits. If you are "in the pink," you are looking well; if you see the world through "rose-colored glasses," then you are optimistic and all is well—"everything's rosy!" Many values of pink are associated with love, romance and tenderness; when blue is added to create lilac-pink, the color takes on an aura of mystery. From deep rose to the sugar colors used to celebrate the birth of a baby girl, pink is also associated with femininity.

Shades of pink bring to mind spring flowers—apple blossom orchards, wild roses and meadow flowers. It is a versatile and easy-to-live with color. Pale tones teamed with soft green or crisp white echo the look of foliage and flowers and give any room a fresh feel, whereas dusky shades of rose or tulip pinks, used with dark green, create a stylish, sophisticated look.

Pink schemes

Pink used skillfully can help you change the mood of a room or adjust the proportions. It is the ideal color to make a large, cold, unwelcoming room look warmer and more inviting. In Victorian rooms with high ceilings, which often seem cold and lofty, you can color the ceiling and the floor dark dusky pink, so the two surfaces appear closer together. Pick out moldings in white or rich cream; teamed with a patterned wallcovering in pale shades of pink with splashes of green, the overall effect will be much more inviting. Alternatively,▶

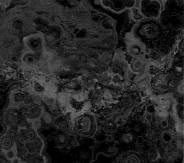

Opulent pinks

In this opulent Regency-style dining room, the elegant decor is based on a wide spectrum of pink tones—striped wallpaper graduates from palest pink through dusky shades to red, while lavish curtains with a bold floral pattern continue the scheme. Cool pistachio green and dark mahogany balance the overall effect.

Spring blossom

Shades of pale pink and crisp white, the colors of spring blossoms, work together to give small rooms a light, fresh look. In this pretty bathroom, delicate floral wallpaper, lace curtains and pillows are the perfect complement for cool, light-reflecting bathroom ceramics. Splashes of green foliage add a vibrant contrast.

Ice-cream shades

Soft ice-cream pink, teamed with the rich raspberry color of the bedcover, the cream and pink shades of the curtains and the chair cover, create a warm glow in this elegant, feminine bedroom.

Color theory

■ Shades of pink are ideal for brightening a monochromatic scheme—a cold, clinical-looking bathroom, for example, with all white equipment and black and white floor tiles. A pale pink ceiling and wall area above the tiles and sharp pink accents introduced in the blind or curtain fabric, will help to add warmth and welcome to the room. Do not forget the decorator's trick of using some contrasting accents and textures to emphasize the overall effect of the scheme—some strong touches of turquoise or a few brass items would work well.

■ Adjacent, or neighborly, color schemes are the most friendly ones to work with; they make use of several segments that lie next to each other on a color wheel. Pink is, in fact, a tint; that is, a full-strength color—red—with white added. On a color wheel made up of tints, pink is next to shades of lilac and mauve. Sugar pink and rose, with pale mauves and lilacs, softened with creamy-whites, can look enchanting in an east-facing bedroom. The curtains and bed linen could be patterned in pinks, magenta, lilacs, purples and deep blue on white to tie the scheme together.

ROBERT HARDING PICTURE LIBRARY – ADAM WOOLFITT

▲ The classic green and pink color scheme, a popular combination for the country-house look, is given an unusual twist here with accents in bold blue. The warm yellow hue of salmon pink works well with the rich mid-blue.

▼ For an exotic look, ideal for transforming an uninspiring hall or landing, combine pale and dusky pink—in color-washed or rag-rolled walls—with cool gray-blue. Add accents in gold or black with neutral wood tones for balance.

ABODE UK

ARCAID – KEN KIRKWOOD

◀ Shades of yellow-pink, apricot and soft rust-orange are next to each other on the warm side of the color wheel, and are therefore known as harmonious colors. Used in this elegant living room, they create a warm, comfortable atmosphere, enhancing the rich, shiny tones of the dark wood furniture and fireplace. Neutral colors—pale browns and beiges, or heavy cream shades and off-whites—also work well with this color scheme.

ROBERT HARDING PICTURE LIBRARY

▲ Clever lighting can enhance the colors in a room, creating a warm, cozy feel. Here, the dusky pink walls are given a warm glow with muted light from the elaborate fixture over the table, while the lamp highlights the side table.

◀ In this light and spacious bedroom, raspberry sorbet pink combines with crisp white to create a bright, fresh scheme. The striking fabric, used on the four-poster bed and as floor-length curtains, makes the most of the room's height.

ELIZABETH WHITING ASSOCIATES

◀ For a striking ethnic-style look, team bright pink with rich shades of orange and blue. Here, a plain, bright pink wall provides the perfect backdrop for bold accessories in rainbow colors. This vibrant and powerful color combination evokes images of hot summer sunshine; rich shades of blue, pink and orange are also popular for creating a Mediterranean look.

ARCAID – RICHARD WAITE

if you have a long, narrow space, such as a corridor, hallway or landing, you can square it up using strong values of pink at each end, partnered with subtle tones of pale pink on the other walls and the ceiling to foreshorten it.

Hot pink schemes

Pastels, ice-cream colors and sugar-almond shades are only part of the pink spectrum. For a stimulating, bold color scheme, team colors such as deep blue, terra-cotta and orange with bold, bright cerise or Provençal pink. This combination is ideal for creating a hot Mediterranean look—use two-thirds bold pink and orange to one-third deep blue for a striking sunny scheme. If, on the other hand, you want to a more balanced feel, reverse the ratios—use one-third bright pink and orange with two-thirds blue. Add natural neutrals—wooden accessories, earthenware and terra-cotta—to complete the look.

Sophisticated pink

For a sophisticated look, warm shades of pink used with cool colors, such as gray or blue-green, are perfect. Careful lighting is important for a scheme that relies on rich colors and bold patterns. The two large windows in this dining room let in a lot of natural light, enhancing the decor, and in the evening, strategically placed lights, table lamps and candles take over, creating a cozy glow rather than harsh, cold illumination.

Dusky pink and red teamed with cool green accents create a sophisticated look.

Soft and sweet

Sugar pink is a popular choice for feminine bedroom schemes and children's rooms as, used with neutral shades, it creates a soft and welcoming look. Elegant furniture—comfortable upholstered chairs in shades of pink, delicately carved cupboards and drawers in mellow wood tones—works best against this backdrop. Lavish bedcoverings and fabric in rich shades of pink add the finishing touch.

For a welcoming scheme, mix sugar pink and raspberry pink with warm wood tones

Fresh shades

Bathrooms can often look cold and clinical, dominated by glossy ceramic surfaces and chrome. Pale pink is an ideal color to balance the shining white and reflects warmly on the skin to give a fresh and healthy glow. Textured accessories— wicker or cane chairs, fluffy towels and bath mats, or even driftwood pieces and plants—all help to counteract the stark, shiny surfaces of a bathroom.

Pale pinks, soft wood tones and green foliage balance cold bathroom ceramics.

ROBERT HARDING PICTURE LIBRARY

ROBERT HARDING PICTURE LIBRARY

ELIZABETH WHITING ASSOCIATES

Luxurious accessories

For dining in style, an elaborate candle-lit chandelier hanging above the table is the perfect accessory; alternatively, you could use elegant brass or silver candlesticks placed at each end of the table—both will create an intimate glow of light. Dusky shades of pink, bold greens and elaborately patterned fabrics are the ideal backdrop for gilt photograph frames and mirror frames. A strategically placed mirror will reflect the candlelight, too. And for side tables and alcove shelves, pretty ornaments—delicate porcelain figures, small vases, trinket boxes, snuff boxes or small silver objects—add the finishing touch.

Hand-crafted styling

Antique-style lace, patchwork quilts and pillow covers, as well as embroidered samplers, all enhance a charming pink bedroom scheme. Drape lace throws casually over comfortable chairs or arrange them on the end of the bed over a brightly colored patchwork quilt. Samplers in pastel shades—particularly the traditional alphabet sampler—are ideal for adults' and children's bedrooms alike. In a child's room, accessories will need to be practical as well as pretty—use washable cotton, rather than antique-style lace, and make sure that any patchwork covers do not need dry cleaning. Old-fashioned children's toys, such as this charming rocking horse, still popular today, will be both decorative and functional.

THE PHOTOGRAPHERS' LIBRARY

MAIN PICTURE AND INSET: CAMERA PRESS, LONDON

Pretty and practical

Comfort and warmth are all-important in a bathroom, and the color scheme and the accessories should enhance these features. Extravagant, deep-pile towels in shades of pink and white, with a decorative border, add texture, warmth and color. And when it comes to choosing bathroom accessories, opt for the glitter of gold instead of chrome to add a warm and opulent touch. If you already have chrome fixtures, add a decorative gold or brass candle sconce or replace your bathroom mirror with a gilt-framed version. Damp-loving plants, such as maidenhair ferns, thrive in a warm, moist bathroom environment and add a splash of vibrant color. Place these plants wherever practical, even on the side of the tub, but preferably out of drafts.

MAIN PICTURE AND INSET, ROBERT HARDING PICTURE LIBRARY

ROBERT HARDING PICTURE LIBRARY

Although they are considered to be noncolors, neutrals are the foundation for many very successful color schemes that are both stylish and, above all, easy to live with.

Neutrals

In terms of color theory, there are only three true neutrals: pure white, black and the various values of pure gray, made by mixing black and white to create different tones. These neutrals can be stark and uninviting, and light-absorbing black can look very somber.

However, beige, off-white, cream and even soft brown are accepted neutrals, as are the colors of natural fibers, grasses, stone, slate and various woods. These are easier to work with but have their own subtle color, which may need careful color-matching.

Never dismiss an existing surface as off-white or safely neutral when you are putting together a color scheme. If you have a cream carpet, cream upholstery or neutral-colored furniture and you combine it with pure white paintwork, or wallcoverings and fabrics with a white ground, you could make the existing item look very dingy!

Color-match as accurately as you can before you buy—ask to borrow a show-length sample or a swatch book, or if all else fails, buy a small piece of fabric or a roll of wallpaper to guard against a more costly mistake.

Using neutrals

Used together, black, white and gray tend to create a modern image. They are often included in stylized geometric patterns, as a monochromatic theme or combined with one or two other strong colors. The stark contrast can add individuality and, according to how the colors are used, can set a style as varied as Art Deco, high-tech, minimalist or metropolitan; but the mixture always needs suitable color accents to avoid looking cold and unwelcoming.

Black and white checkerboard flooring was much used in classical architecture of the 17th and 18th century; black, white and gray, offset with terra-cotta for warmth, is a distinctly 18th century color combination; black used with gold and yellow, or another strong shade, such as jade or Indian red, has a Regency flavor. ▶

Warm creams

Walls in a warm mottled neutral color, set off with a white ceiling and drapes, create a sophisticated atmosphere with the contrasting black of the cast iron fireplace and the classic gold fleur-de-lis motifs on the wall. Like the swallowtail butterfly wing, color interest comes in a single splash of orangy yellow.

ROBERT HARDING PICTURE LIBRARY – MICHAEL BROCKWAY; INSET, ROBERT HARDING PICTURE LIBRARY

Accepted neutrals

Off-whites, creams, beiges and gray-beiges are often found in natural products— stone, sand, wood, cork, natural fibers— and give vital textural interest to schemes using blander shades.

True neutrals

This dining room with its basic scheme of pure black and white has an exotic look, created by the oriental prints, the designs on the chair backs and the shining black of the chairs and table. Color accent comes from the rich, polished finish of the inlaid wood tabletop—a natural golden tiger color—and the flowers and foliage.

Color theory

■ Many people find natural/neutral schemes the most comfortable and easy to live with, but they can be very bland and safe. The overall effect is usually monochromatic (different values of one color); so if schemes are to be successful, you need plenty of textural contrast as well as the addition of interesting accents.

■ "Hints of" and "tints of" colors are really very pale values of pink, greens, yellows, lilac, blue and peach, so relate back to the original colors in the spectrum, lightened and watered down with white. These need careful color-matching and can be disappointing in use, as they tend to be very pale in tonal value. If you have a mix of tints, you will need to relate the color back to the original hue, perhaps deepening it to create a monochromatic (tone-on-tone) scheme, which you can cheer up with some contrasting accents.

■ When matching colors with samples, remember to look at them in the right plane—vertical for wall and window treatments and horizontal for carpets. Check how they look in both natural daylight and as they will be lit at night, too; some colors can look quite different when viewed under artificial light.

ABODE UK

ROBERT HARDING PICTURE LIBRARY

▲ Based on soft, mushroomy neutrals, this breakfast-room with its wheat-colored walls and oatmeal carpet has light and space but is still warm. Polished pine, the open hearth and touches of shiny metal in the coal scuttle and picture frames provide textural contrast.

▼ It is a brave decorator who will base a room scheme on dark gray and black, but the effect in this late-Victorian-style room is surprisingly warm. Color and textural accents are the key, with shining wood and stone orbs, fire surround and eclectic accessories to add interest.

Touches of black sharpen up a color scheme more than any pure color, but black can strobe (lines or patterns appear to float, making you feel dizzy) or create a hard edge. Use black as an accessory color or to emphasize a feature, but remember to balance it with a little white or a very pale tint.

Pale grays are a good contrasting accent for a dark or very warm scheme, and mixed with lavenders, mauves and purple will create a sophisticated ambience. Deeper grays work well with pale minty greens, turquoise, lemon and peach, and contrast effectively with most colors in their lighter tones.

White can look bland or stark on its own, but if used in light-reflecting or light-filtering textures, such as lace, ceramic tiles, muslin, etched glass, damask or gloss paint, it will add interest and depth while enhancing the existing scheme.

ABODE UK

ROBERT HARDING PICTURE LIBRARY – TOM LEIGHTON

◄ Black and white or off-white combinations do not need to look stark or geometric. The naive animal paintings on the upholstery add an eye-catching touch in an otherwise very simply decorated room.

▶ Neutrals that tend toward warm yellow are easy to live with but need contrasts to prevent them from being bland. Rich wood furniture and accessories in plum, terra-cotta and shades of beige to brown highlight this large, open living room.

◄ Shiny black and white, even with the help of a warm wood floor and the gleam of chrome fittings, can look very plain and institutional. For most people, this minimalist approach to bathroom decor cries out for some color, some warmth and, most of all, something to break up the huge expanse of white wall!

▲ This monochromatic scheme of natural neutrals explores the full potential of textures, such as stone, whitewash, quarry tiles, nubby untreated wool and wood. This scheme will suit all seasons—add color accents of flowers in bright colors for autumn and winter, and fresh, lighter tones for summer and spring.

Classic designs

Most creams tend to be yellowish (and tend to yellow even more with age), so they work like pale yellow, warming up a room scheme and adding a touch of sunshine. A plain background with just a soft mottling of color is an ideal setting for some unusual matching accessories with dramatic impact; but be sure to add some real color, such as the aqua pillows, to prevent the overall scheme from looking flat.

Gold, cream and black are elegant, fashionable and sophisticated.

Country colors

Matching walls and ceiling, painted in a flat near-white color, are the best way of accentuating the feeling of space in a room that has small corners or alcoves or, as in this section of a living room/hallway, has a wedge-shaped area under the stairs. Natural wood, wicker and the warm russet colors of the rug add the necessary color and texture in an otherwise starkly decorated room.

Cream, woody colors and a touch of greeny-gray give a look of rustic comfort.

Ebony black

Pure black and pure white—the truest of neutrals—create the strongest of all contrasts. Essentially this is a white room with black furniture and a stone gray carpet, but the finished effect is sophisticated and pleasing to the eye. The large expanse of white wall is broken up by the outlines of unusually shaped oriental-style ornaments and by the highly polished walnut inlay on the top of the dining table.

The black, white and gold of tiger markings create a bold color scheme.

CHAPTER 3

Color Effects in Your Home

Easy to master, these stunning paint effects **add texture and depth of color to walls and accessories—**all in a matter of hours. **Follow these simple steps to discover the** speed and versatility **of flogging, paper texturing and wet sponging.**

Quick
paint
effects

Like other paint and glaze techniques, flogging, paper texturing and wet sponging will add eye-catching texture to almost any surface—walls, woodwork and accessories. There are no complex steps or special skills to learn. It takes just two or three easy stages to create patterns and textures in a wet top coat of oil-based glaze or satin-finish latex paint. The materials are cheap and simple too: a natural sponge, sheets of paper or a long-haired brush.

In this pretty floral room, left, all three techniques were coordinated, but there is no limit to the colors you can use. Mix and match colors to suit any style or look, from country to Regency. These easy effects can add visual interest and texture in any room.

Getting started

With proper preparation, these paint effects are suitable for walls, woodwork and accessories. If the surface you wish to decorate has already been painted, sand with coarse sandpaper, then fine-grade sandpaper. For walls and woodwork, sand any flaking plaster or wood until the surface is smooth. With laminates or ceramics, first sand, then apply a layer of all-purpose primer.

YOU WILL NEED:

- I quart each satin latex paint in cream and pink
- Two medium-sized paintbrushes
- Masking tape
- Scissors
- Large sheets of paper (see text)

Paper texturing

Paper texturing is one of the cheapest paint effects you can do—all you need is paper and two colors of satin-finish latex paint to add exciting textures to walls and accessories.

Sometimes known as *frottage,* this technique involves rubbing creased paper squares against a layer of wet satin-finish paint. When the paper is removed, a texture similar to crushed velvet appears as some of the top color is removed to reveal the base color beneath.

The pattern you create will vary according to the type of paper you use. The overall texture and the amount of base coat revealed depends on the absorbency and thickness of the paper, and how hard you rub the paper will also influence the pattern. Newspaper has the right texture and absorbency, but be careful that the newsprint does not come off on the paint.

1 Mask off the chair rail

● Clean the chair rail and dry thoroughly. Apply masking tape along the full length of the rail, both above and below it. To stop any paint from seeping onto the walls, press the masking tape down firmly.

2 Painting the base coat

● Apply an even coat of the cream paint along the whole chair rail, using horizontal brushstrokes. Allow to dry (this will take 2–4 hours).

3 Preparing the paper

● Cut the large sheets of paper into squares of roughly the same size. This size can vary depending on the size of the job at hand (see Tips, right). Gently scrunch up each square into a loose ball, then lightly smooth it out with your fingers so that the paper is still slightly crumpled and the creases are still clearly visible.

TIPS

■ **Vary the size of the paper squares you use** according to your needs. If your chair rail is very narrow, cut the squares so that they are only fractionally wider than the depth of the chair rail itself.

■ If you are working on a large area, do not be tempted to make the paper squares too large. The pattern made by the paper will become too irregular and the effect will be spoiled. Keep to smaller squares and work in blocks over the surface.

■ If, when you peel back the paper, too much or too little paint has been removed, repaint with the top color of satin latex and redo the technique.

■ Paper texturing can be used on most surfaces, flat or curved. When applying the paper, make sure you mold the paper around all contours and corners.

■ As there is only a thin coating of paint left after paper texturing, this technique dries very quickly. Although it will be touch dry after about one hour, let the surface dry for up to four hours before repositioning any furniture.

4 Painting the top coat

● Using a medium-sized paintbrush, apply an even coat of pink. Satin-finish latex paint starts to dry and becomes unworkable after only a few minutes, so apply the top coat in strips only slightly longer than the square of paper you use.

5 Texturing with the paper

● Working quickly, lay one of the paper squares along the chair rail so that the rail is completely covered from top to bottom. Gently rub the paper smooth by running your fingers from the center to the edge of the paper square. The harder you rub, the more of the top coat will be removed.

6 Peel back the paper

● Carefully and slowly peel away the paper square. The paper is now wet, so make sure it does not rip as you remove it. Do not leave the paper on the chair rail for too long because, as the paint dries, the paper will become stuck to the surface.

EQUIPMENT

YOU WILL NEED:
- 1 quart each oil-based paint in pink and cream
- 1 quart oil-based glaze
- Paint thinner
- Two large paintbrushes
- Flogging brush
- Masking tape
- Scissors
- Paint pail
- Mixing sticks
- Lint-free rags

Flogging

Flogging is a subtractive glaze technique that gives an effect not unlike that of fine-grained wood. This paint effect is easy to master, and in two very simple stages, you can add a soft texturing to walls, accessories and furniture.

The all-important piece of equipment is a long-bristled flogging brush, which produces a close grainy texture as you slap it against a coating of wet glaze in a series of upward movements. This impact causes the long bristles of the brush to splay out slightly, giving a grainy texture to the glaze, which allows the color of the base coat to show through.

The subtle uniform texture makes flogging ideal for any large flat surfaces. Muted colors work best with large surfaces, although more striking color combinations can brighten up smaller items.

1 Apply the base coat

● Mask off the chair rail and cornice or ceiling, and apply a base coat of pink oil-based paint, using a large paintbrush. Let dry—this will take at least 12–16 hours.

2 Mixing the glaze

● Pour some cream oil-based paint and oil-based glaze into a paint pail and stir well. The consistency needs to be like that of light cream (see Help File, right).

3 Applying the top coat

● When the glaze mixture is the right consistency, apply it over the dry pink base, using a large paintbrush in long, even brushstrokes. Work in strips so that the glaze does not start to dry (see Help File, right.)

4 Laying off the glaze

● To even out the layer of glaze and to eliminate the brush marks, lightly drag the paintbrush down the glaze in one continuous movement. If the glaze does not spread evenly in certain areas, apply a little more glaze and smooth it out again.

! As with all techniques that use oil-based glaze, remember to lay out glaze-soaked rags to dry completely before you dispose of them. Glaze has a very low flash point, and can sometimes spontaneously combust if rags are left to dry scrunched up in the trash can.

5 Flogging the top coat

● Starting at the bottom and moving slowly upward, slap the flogging brush against the glaze in even, slightly overlapping strips. Never drag the brush—it must be raised up and slapped down briskly as you work up the wall.

6 Wipe off the excess

● The brush will soon be saturated with glaze, so wipe excess glaze off the bristles with a lint-free cloth at regular intervals (see the cautionary tip, above).

7 Flogging around the edges

● Corners and areas around the cornice, baseboard or chair rail are hard to reach with a flogging brush. Instead, take an ordinary paintbrush and use it to texture these areas in the same way.

Wet sponging

Wet sponging is quick and easy. By sponging on a base of wet tinted glaze, the top and base colors blend together to give a soft texture like fossilized marble.

There is no need to wait for layers of oil-based paint to dry—the whole paint effect is completed while the base coat is still wet.

YOU WILL NEED:

- 2½ quarts satin-finish oil-based paint in cream
- 1 quart satin-finish oil-based paint in each of three shades of pink
- 1 quart oil-based glaze
- Paint thinner
- Medium-sized paintbrush
- Natural sponge
- Paint pail
- Mixing sticks
- Three plastic plates
- Masking tape
- Scissors

The above quantities are sufficient to cover the walls of a 12' x 15' room.

1 Mixing the base coat

- Pour some of the cream paint into a paint pail and add twice as much oil-based glaze. Stir thoroughly until the consistency is smooth and the color is evenly distributed throughout the mixture.

2 Preparing the pinks

- Pour a small amount of each of the three pink paint colors onto three plastic plates. Do not overfill the plates, or the paint will spill over the edge when you dip the sponge into it.

3 Applying the glaze

● Load a paintbrush with the glaze mixture and apply evenly over the wall. Work in 3' strips so that the glaze does not become unworkable.

4 Loading the sponge

● Load the sponge generously with the mid-pink paint. You will need more than for normal sponging as the wet base coat will absorb a lot of the colors sponged over the top of it.

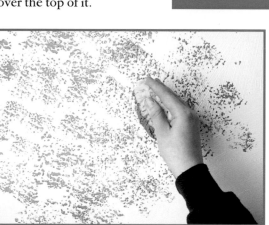

5 Start sponging

● Working quickly while the base coat is still wet, sponge on the mid-tone pink paint in a random pattern. Apply liberally so that the cream base color does not dominate the overall effect.

6 Light pink sponging

● Wipe off the excess paint from the sponge, then load it with the lightest pink color. Working over the first color, sponge in a dabbing action to build up an even distribution of texture. You have to work quickly as the base will start to dry.

7 Dark pink sponging

● Finally, sponge on the darkest pink paint. Apply sparingly; otherwise, it will overpower the other colors. Once you are satisfied with the overall effect, allow to dry for 12–16 hours before repositioning furniture or wall hangings.

■ Wet sponging works best with several tones of the same color, as they will blend together to give a gently mottled appearance. However, for a more striking look, try contrasting colors, such as yellow, pale blue and dark blue. If the colors are very bright, confine the effect to a small area to avoid it looking too dazzling.

■ The texture of flogging is very subtle, so it is important to get the color combination right. A dark base color will produce a more striking grainy effect than the other way around.

■ Always test your choice of colors for flogging before embarking on a project, as the two colors will change when they are placed on top of each other. If the colors are too similar, the base coat will not be visible and the graining effect will be lost.

■ The base coat for paper texturing can be either lighter or darker than the top coat, depending on the effect you wish to create. For the best and most striking effect, select two contrasting colors in different tones.

● The walls in this room
have been sponged with
a natural sponge, using
pale peach and cream
over a solid painted base
of light orange. The
appearance is feathery
and light, and the
colors blend together.
Generally, the more
diluted your paint, the
softer and less distinct
your sponged effect will
be. By varying the
pressure and thickness of
the paint you use, you
can create different
textures and patterns.

Even if you have never attempted any decorating **more adventurous than a coat of flat or gloss latex paint, you can achieve wonderful color effects with sponging—the simplest of all paint techniques.**

Sponging

Essentially, sponging is a technique that uses several colors—applied randomly, one over another with a loose-textured sponge—to produce a speckled effect, and the color combinations are limitless. The naturally springy and open texture of sea sponges first inspired the technique. Natural sponge is ideal for the job, but you can simulate the effect, using a synthetic sponge, at a fraction of the cost.

Sponging know-how

Experiment with colors to create the look you want, using gentle, toning pastels or vibrant, vivid contrasts. For plain walls—sheetrock or plaster—sponging with ordinary latex paint gives a quick and easy face-lift. But other surfaces, such as wood, ceramics, glass or laminates, also lend themselves to the sponging treatment. All you need are the appropriate paints.

Color choice

The great advantage of sponging is that you can vary the degree to which any color dominates the effect—and it is easy to alter the appearance as you work. The base color can show through the sponging as much—or as little—as you like.

When choosing a color scheme for a room, you can create a subtle coordinated effect by picking up a color from the upholstery or curtains to use as a sponged layer. To extend the effect, use the same colors in a different order to sponge

accessories, such as lamps or shelves.

One color sponged over a background will give quite a naive, unsophisticated effect that may not always be suitable, whereas two layers create subtle clouded or speckled shading—and it takes little extra time to add a second sponging.

Getting started

The step-by-step instructions show how to build up a sponged pattern, but it is always worth doing an experimental piece before you begin. Even if you are sure of how you want your colors to combine, try out different degrees of pressure on a piece of paper. If you are too heavy-handed, the texture will be flattened out of the sponge, and you will get blotchy patches with no detail; too little pressure, and you will only get a sparse dotting effect. While this may be ideal for a final touch with a very bold color, it does not give sufficient color for most purposes.

When you have gauged the right pressure, continue to dab, moving the angle of the sponge around all the time to give a completely random effect with no hint of a repeating pattern, as this would detract from the allover appearance.

PHOTOGRAPHY BY LIZZIE ORME

YOU WILL NEED:
- 2½ quarts flat latex paint in base color
- I quart flat latex paint in first sponging color
- I quart flat latex paint in second sponging color
- Roller and brush
- Natural or synthetic sponge
- Paint tray
- Paint pail
- Masking tape
- Scissors
- Paper for testing
The above paint quantities are sufficient for a 12' x 15' room.

◀ In this blue room, turquoise green and pale blue have been sponged over deep cornflower, using a synthetic sponge. The individual colors are easier to define than when applied with a natural sponge.

The overall effect

If you are only sponging a small area, it is easy to keep sight of the whole effect—but if you are dealing with a whole room, you may find that you have accidentally changed the pressure of your sponging as you progress. Stand back from the walls at intervals and make sure that the sponged texture is even and not patchy. Always complete one color of sponging before you go on to the next one, and try to finish each layer of sponging in one session so as to keep the pressure as consistent as possible.

Cleaning up

If you are using water-based paint, all you need to do to clean your sponge is wipe off excess paint on absorbent paper, then wash the sponge thoroughly in running water with a little soap.

If you have been using an oil-based paint, pour a little paint thinner into a bowl and squeeze the sponge in it to remove most of the paint. Wash the sponge in warm soapy water, continuing to rinse the sponge until the water is clean. Let the sponge dry naturally in a spot where air can circulate around it.

PHOTOGRAPHY BY LIZZIE ORME

 Remember to buy flat—not satin finish—latex paint for sponging; the sheen on satin-finish paint would detract from the soft, blended appearance of the sponging. Similarly, on surfaces that require an oil-based treatment, use flat oil-based paint, available in fast-drying acrylic form.

1 Preparation

● Make sure your walls are absolutely smooth, filling and sanding down any cracks, then cleaning the walls to remove any dust and grease. Use an all-purpose cleaner or warm soapy water.

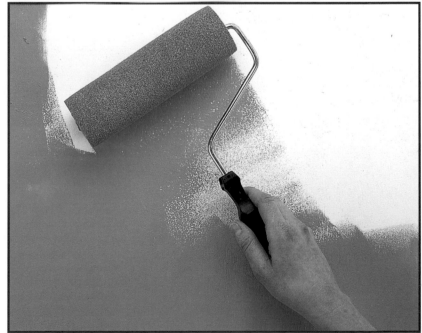

● When the walls are dry, mask off edges abutting the ceiling and baseboard with tape to ensure a clean finish, then apply the base color. Unless you are covering a dark color with a lighter one, you will probably only need to give the walls one coat of the base color. If you are using a roller, use a small brush to fill in edges and corners. Allow to dry—this may take up to 4 hours, depending on room temperature.

2 Preparing the sponge

● To adapt a sponge, use sharp scissors to cut away the corners and edges of a loose-textured, springy household sponge to make a soft, oval shape. Snip out pieces from one flat face of the sponge, using the tips of the scissors, and use your thumb and forefinger to pinch out more tiny pieces. Repeat this on a small piece of sponge to use in corners and on edges.
● Mix the paint for the first sponged layer. When using water-based paint, mix equal quantities of paint and water together in a paint pail. The thinned paint should be the consistency of light cream so that it gives a soft-edged print.

3 Picking up paint

● When you are ready to start, pour the diluted paint into a tray and tip the tray until the paint covers the slanting roller section. Soften the sponge with a little water, then dip the prepared sponge face into the paint remaining on the roller section.

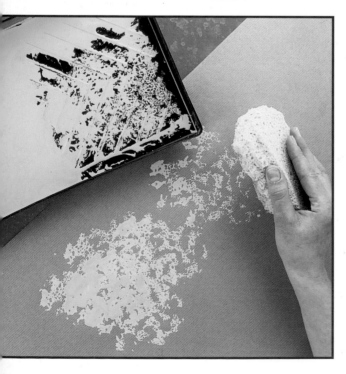

● Dab off the excess paint on a piece of paper; it is important to do this to prevent the sponged effect from being too blotchy when you make the first dabs with the sponge. Test the texture on the paper, trying different degrees of pressure until you produce a look you like. Practice rotating the sponge as you dab to give a varied impression. To ensure an even effect, you will need to dab off excess paint every time you reload your sponge, so try to pick up only a little paint at a time to avoid waste.

4 Sponging

● Start sponging on the walls, working from one top corner downward and outward. You will probably find that you can make several prints before you need to reload your sponge with paint. Keep turning the sponge to vary the impression you make. Finish the whole room with the first color. For corners and edges, see the steps opposite.
● Rinse the sponge in warm water until it is completely clean and squeeze out excess water. When the sponging is dry, mix the second sponging color and apply in the same way. As before, keep the pressure even and alter the angle of the sponge to ensure a random effect. Stand back from the finished walls to see if any area looks uneven or needs touching up.

5 Corners

● Do not try to sponge into corners or up to edges with the large sponge; for these areas, use the small piece of prepared sponge. Work on one side of the corner first, rolling and dabbing the sponge into the angle, varying the way you hold it as you go. Let that side dry, then sponge the other side in the same way.

● Mask around light switches with tape, making sure enough tape stands up around the edges to protect the switch. Sponge up to the edge of the switch, rolling the sponge into the corner and varying the angle to keep an even, random cover.

● When sponging near the ceiling, hold a piece of firm cardboard against the masked angle of the ceiling to shield the plain paintwork. Dab excess paint from the sponge as described before, and use a slight rocking movement to roll the small piece of sponge into the angle. Keep moving the piece of cardboard along as you work, wiping the edge frequently so that you do not smear wet paint from the cardboard onto the ceiling.

Windows

● Rolls of specially designed masking paper are available to protect wide areas. Once you have stuck the tape along the edge you wish to mask, fold out the flap of paper, which doubles the width of the area masked. In the corners of windowsills, sponge one side of the angle at a time, as above. Use the small sponge to dab paint into the corner, rolling it into the angle. Allow the first side of the corner to dry before sponging the second, so you can wipe away any blotches without smearing the wet sponging.

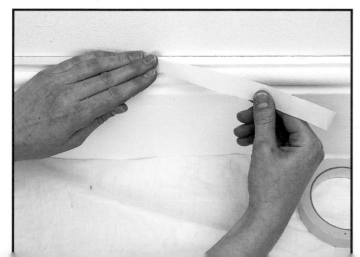

Edges

● To sponge up to edges abutting baseboards or window frames, make sure that the edges are masked securely with low-tack tape. (If you find the tape is too sticky, reduce the tackiness by pressing it on a piece of cloth before applying it to the paintwork.) Sponge up to the tape, rolling the sponge in the same way as for a masked switch so that the sponge reaches right to the edge.

■ If, when you stand back, there appear to be blotches, break up the effect by sponging over the area with a different color. Similarly, if you feel that the base color has been lost under the sponging, dilute some of the base color and sponge the patchy area again, this time pressing only lightly.

■ You do not necessarily have to repaint a room to sponge it. For an instant face-lift, make sure the walls are completely clean, then sponge directly over the existing paint.

■ Start sponging in areas that are most likely to be obscured by furniture; this way, your most practiced sponging will be the most obvious.

SURFACES
Sponging is a very versatile technique and, using either water- or oil-based paint, is suited to most surfaces, including fine or rough plaster, cork tiling, curved walls, glass, ceramics, stone, brickwork, vinyl floor tiles, painted woodwork, metal, concrete, woodchip and laminated surfaces.

DRYING TIME
Depending on temperature, sponged latex paint takes up to two hours; oil-based paint, up to 10 hours.

DESIGN ideas

Color combinations for sponging are as limitless as your imagination—and any room in the house can be given a lift by sponging.

■ Why settle for one plain color, when you can create a subtle sponged effect with two or three different ones, matched to tone with your upholstery, curtains and even the furniture?

Sponging gives a much more pleasing effect than a plain painted surface—it is as good as wallpaper, but less expensive and more flexible. Experiment with different techniques, sponging some areas more intensely than others to give a distinct clouded effect, as in the bathroom opposite, or keeping the texture soft and the contrasts gentle, as in the dining room corner below.

The sponged rooms shown here provide a few ideas of how to combine colors for the most interesting effects. Make up some color swatches as a guide when working out the color scheme. Sponging is the easiest way possible to create your own designer wallcovering.

■ Although apparently clashing colors can be combined with eye-catching effects, for the most subtle look, use paints in shades or tints of the same color. A particularly harmonious sponged effect comes from using only two colors but blending the two together for the second layer of sponging.

◀ The sponging below this bathroom shelf has been deliberately worked in patches to give a clouded, watery effect, rather like drifting seaweed. A base of pale turquoise has been sponged in random patches with dark blue, then all over in darker turquoise.

▶ A background of cream gives a softer effect when sponged over than a background of stark white. This country kitchen was painted in a warm, yellowy cream, then a first layer of sponging was added in a soft chalky mauve. A pale turquoise blue sponged very lightly over the top in a less regular, patchy pattern gives a pretty, shaded look.

◀ Only by looking closely at these walls can you tell that they are sponged—but the effect is softer and more subtle than plain paint. This effect is achieved by using colors that are quite similar—a cream base with a hint of apricot blends with sponging in two shades of peachy orange. The appearance is very warm and fresh, and complements the rich browns of the fireplace mantel and tile, the tablecloth and the chairs.

PHOTOGRAPHY BY GRAHAM RAE

SPONGING
other surfaces

■ Sponging is an ideal technique for accessorizing small pieces of furniture or decorative items to tone with your color scheme. It is important to prepare any surface that you want to sponge so that the paint will adhere to it. For untreated wood, sand down thoroughly and paint with a wood primer before painting. On existing gloss paintwork, sand down well and use oil-based or acrylic paint for the base and the sponging. Treat metals with red oxide metal primer; this takes about 24 hours to dry, so allow plenty of time before painting. On glazed pottery or glass, use specialized ceramic paint and follow the maker's instructions; paint unglazed pottery with latex paint, which will adhere to the rough surface.

▶ This sponged metal pot used to have a shiny, galvanized finish. For an easy makeover, we painted it with red oxide metal primer to prevent rusting and to provide a surface for the paint to adhere to, then gave it a coat of deep purple paint. (A light color would need two coats of paint to cover over the red oxide.) After sponging in a light mauve, the pot was sprayed with a clear matte varnish as a protective finish.

▲ The unglazed ceramic base of the lamp was painted with a rich cream-colored latex paint, then sponged over with a deep terra-cotta color. The second layer of sponging was added in a mixture of the two colors. The paper shade was painted in the same terra-cotta paint used on the base, then very lightly sponged with the same cream, blended with a little terra-cotta. The effect is a translucent wispy pattern, which, while toning with the lamp base, is less busy and has gentler color contrasts.

Stippling

Teenagers are always on the lookout for something new and individual—and this stippled bedroom is both. We have combined light and dark stippling to create a dramatic striped effect.

Stippling

There are two types of stippling: soft and coarse. And although each type gives a finish where one paint color shows through another, each produces a different look. A soft stippling brush gives a fine, freckled appearance, whereas the coarse technique with a plastic stippler leaves a more grainy texture.

Most flat surfaces are suitable for stippling, as long as there are no lumps, bumps or uneven spots. Even minor flaws tend to be emphasized by the subtle texture of stippling. The other requirement is a firm, steady hand. It is essential to apply the glaze evenly in order to give a consistent result throughout.

Stippling can be quite tiring and is better done in pairs, with one person applying the glaze and the other stippling it off. Don't swap roles halfway, as each person's stippling technique is different, and the finish will lack continuity.

The technique

The finish is achieved by starting with a base coat of oil-based paint, applying a colored glaze over the top and working on the glaze with a stippling brush. The brush is bounced over the wet glaze, leaving spots through which the base coat shows. Remember that, as with all glaze techniques, if you make a mistake, you can wipe it off and start again.

Before you start

Bristle stippling brushes are expensive but worth it in the long run; choose one large enough for the job at hand. Otherwise, use any flat-ended brush, such as a shoe brush, or tie two large paintbrushes together to create a similar effect.

Practice on some cardboard before you begin, then start working on an area that will be hidden by furniture; your technique will improve the longer you work at it. Leave really conspicuous areas until last, for your most practiced work.

YOU WILL NEED:

- I quart oil-based glaze
- Artist's oil colors (blue and white)
- I quart paint thinner
- Paintbrush
- Coarse plastic stippler
- Mixing dishes
- Mixing sticks
- Paint pail
- Cleaning cloth
- Lint-free rag
- Wide masking tape
- Tape measure
- Pencil
- Plumb line

The quantities given are sufficient for a 12' x 15' room.

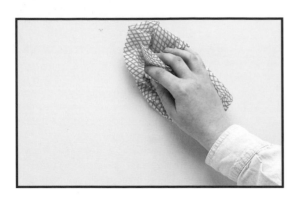

1 Preparation

● Wipe down the oil-base-painted wall with a damp cloth and a mild household cleaner to completely remove any grease and dust.

2 Mask the baseboard

● Using the masking tape, mask the baseboard (and the cornice) to protect from the glaze.

3 Measure the stripes

● Measure along the masked-off cornice and make small pencil marks on the masking tape at 12" intervals.

4 Hang the plumb line

● Hang the plumb line from each mark and make a slight pencil mark at intervals down the length of the string.

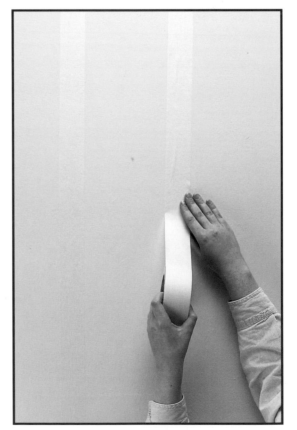

5 Mark the stripes

● Using wide masking tape, mask on the right-hand and left-hand sides of the pencil marks to reveal alternate strips. The masking tape should fall on the inside of the yellow stripes (that is, those that are not being painted) so that none of the stripes to be stippled are covered by masking tape.

6 Color the glaze

● Mix some blue artist's oil color with paint thinner to dissolve it, then blend into the glaze, mixing enough for the whole job. Remember that the color will become paler when stippled.

7 Apply the glaze

● Brush the glaze evenly over every fourth stripe in a thin, even coating, working vertically from top to bottom.

8 Stipple the glaze

● Dab the coarse stippler lightly and evenly over the glaze to create a stippled effect (right). Work down each stripe from top to bottom. Wipe the brush on a cloth from time to time to prevent clogging.

9 Mix the dark glaze

● When you have finished the lighter stripes, add a little diluted blue oil color to the remaining glaze and mix well. Add paint thinner as necessary to keep the glaze workable.

10 Paint the dark stripes

● Apply the darker glaze evenly over the central stripes between the lighter blue stippled stripes. Again, keep the brush-strokes thin and even, and work in a vertical direction.

11 Stipple the dark glaze

● Stipple the stripes as before, wiping the brush on a cloth when necessary.

12 Remove the tape

● Allow the glaze to dry (14–16 hours or overnight). Carefully peel off the masking tape. Touch up places where the paint comes away.

TIPS

■ Never let the glaze get too thick—it should be the consistency of light cream. Thin it with paint thinner until you have the right consistency.

■ As the technique is tiring, work on only

one section at a time—a comfortable arm's span is ideal.

■ Try to finish the project in a day; otherwise, cover the glaze with plastic wrap.

IDEAS

■ Test different base colors with different glazes before deciding on your final scheme.

■ When you are more proficient, try a more complicated surface, like a rounded vase, but only if the surface is completely smooth.

Stippled CD stand

A stereo or CD stand is a perfect candidate for stippling, as all the surfaces and edges are flat. We used a soft stippling brush to achieve a more subtle effect for furniture. You could try stippling a desk, a chair or a bookcase—if all the surfaces are flat, the effects will be spectacular.

EQUIPMENT

- Oil-based paint
- Oil-based glaze
- Artist's oil colors
- Paint thinner
- Paintbrush
- Soft stippling brush
- Fine-grade sandpaper
- Paint pail
- Mixing bowls
- Mixing sticks
- Lint-free cloth

1 Prepare the surfaces

● Make sure the surface is free from grease by wiping down with an all-purpose cleaner. Let dry, then sand lightly so the paint will adhere.

2 Apply the oil-based paint

● Paint all surfaces of the unit in your chosen color of paint. Allow to dry for 12–14 hours.

3 Apply the glaze

● Mix the glaze to the color you want (see step 6 on page 94), then apply in light, even brushstrokes down the length of the edges and horizontally across the top.

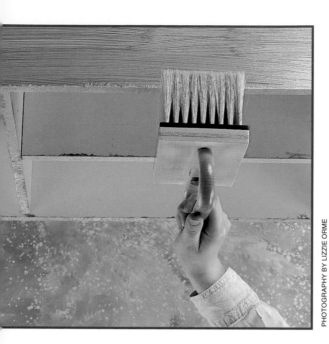

PHOTOGRAPHY BY LIZZIE ORME

4 Stipple the edges

● Using the stippling brush, stipple all the edges of the unit, cleaning the brush on the lint-free cloth from time to time to prevent the bristles from becoming clogged with excess glaze.

6 Clean up any smudges

● When you have finished stippling the whole unit, wipe away any glaze that has smeared onto the plain surface of the shelves, using a rag moistened with paint thinner.

5 Stipple the top

● Stipple the top of the unit, using the stippling brush in a light, even pouncing motion.

Experiment with the fashionable textures **of rag rolling, using** water-based scumble glaze **for a quick and easy** two-color technique.

Rag rollin

PHOTOGRAPHY BY LIZZIE ORME

Bring one of the classic paint techniques up to date, using the increasingly popular—and now widely available—water-based acrylic scumble glaze. Apart from conforming to today's call for decorating materials to be more environmentally friendly, water-based scumble is nonflammable, has no lingering odor, dries more quickly than the oil-based equivalent and does not become discolored with age.

Use water-based materials for both the background paint and the glaze, so that drying times will be considerably shorter than if you were to use oil-based paint and glaze. The only other particular requirement is to use a lint-free cloth; you will probably need a cloth that is the size of a double bed sheet to rag roll a whole room.

Ragging on and off

The technique can be used in two ways: ragging off, where you brush on the glaze, then lift it off as you roll the rag over the glaze; and ragging on, where you apply the glaze directly from a scrunched-up rag.

YOU WILL NEED:

- 2½ quarts flat latex paint in off-white
- 2 quarts acrylic scumble glaze
- 1 quart flat latex paint in each of pale gray and light blue (Very little latex paint is needed to color the glaze, so buy a small can when possible.)
- Two paintbrushes
- Lint-free cloth (see step 1)
- Two large paint pails
- Measuring cup
- Mixing stick
- Tape measure
- Pencil
- Plumb line
- 1½"-wide masking tape
- Scissors
- Rubber gloves

These quantities are sufficient for a 12' x 15' room.

g

1 Cutting up the cloth

● Cut the lint-free cloth into 24" squares. You will need about a double bed sheet's worth to deal with a 12' x 15' room. This is roughly equal to 3 or 4 yards of fabric.

2 Painting the wall

● Apply an even coat of off-white flat latex paint. If painting over a dark color, you will need to give the walls two coats.

3 Coloring the glazes

● Pour 1 quart scumble glaze into a paint pail; add some gray flat latex paint, stirring well, until you get the color you want. The glaze should have the consistency of thin cream; if it does not, dilute with a little water, stirring continuously. Repeat the procedure to mix the blue glaze.

4 Mask lines

● Starting 6" along the cornice from one corner, make pencil marks every 12". Hang a plumb line from each point and make pencil marks down to the chair rail (or baseboard). Apply masking tape down the right side of each pencil line.

Ragging on

5 Loading the cloth

● Scrunch up a piece of cut cloth into a loose bundle and dip into the blue glaze. Now wring out the excess glaze, so that the rag is saturated but not dripping with colored glaze. This is rather messy, so wear rubber gloves.

6 Scrunching up the cloth

● Unfold the glaze-soaked cloth and gently refold it into a loose bundle. The rag should form a loose scrunched-up sausage shape with plenty of random folds to give a varied texture to the finished effect.

7 Ragging on

● Working from the chair rail (or baseboard) upward, place the cloth on the wall and roll it up, occasionally changing direction but keeping an even pressure. Work over alternate stripes.

8 Filling in the spaces

● Stand back from the finished rag rolling and if there are any areas without texture, dab lightly with a scrunched-up cloth that has been loaded with glaze. Only fill in large gaps, so as not to spoil the overall pattern.

Rag rolling on creates a crisp, quite clearly defined texture against a plain background.

HELP FILE

■ If you find that your rag rolling makes too regular a pattern and tends to skid, you probably have rolled the cloth too tightly.

Wipe the surface clean, loosen the crumpling of the piece of cloth and start again.

SURFACES
Rag rolling offers a good disguise for not-quite-perfect walls, so it is not only ideal for good plaster, textured wallpaper, cork wall tiles, glass, laminates and metal (given appropriate priming), but it is also ideal for rough plaster finishes too. Avoid using the technique on curved walls, floorboards, stone or brickwork.

Although the appearance of rag rolling on and off is random, it needs to be even. Always work in an upward direction, rolling the cloth away from yourself in short, diagonal rolls. Never roll down the wall, toward yourself. This is awkward to do and will look blotchy and uneven.

9 Repeating with the gray

● Repeat steps 5 to 7, using fresh pieces of cloth and the gray-tinted glaze. Rag roll over alternate stripes as before, again working from the bottom upward and altering the direction to vary the pattern. Fill in the spaces by dabbing, as before.

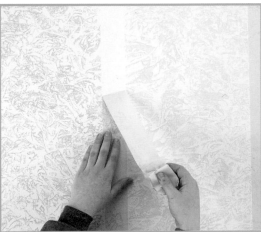

10 Removing the tape

● Gently peel away the masking tape between the ragged-on stripes, leaving the tape along the chair rail. If this has been very heavily covered with glaze, peel away and replace with fresh tape before continuing with the ragging off.

101

Ragging off

The texture of ragging off is subtle; there is always a slight covering of glaze to prevent the background from looking too stark.

11 Applying the glaze

● To give a different texture to the area below the chair rail, apply an even coat of gray-tinted glaze over the base color, working on a strip no wider than 3' at a time to avoid the glaze drying and becoming unworkable.

12 Laying off the glaze

● To create an even base for the rag rolling, finish off the glazed area, using vertical brushstrokes. The glaze must not become too dry for ragging off.

13 Ragging off

● Loosely crumple up a piece of clean cloth and shape it into a short sausage. Working from the bottom up, roll it up the glazed area, altering the angle of the roll as you go. Ideally, one person should apply and lay off the glaze and a second should rag it off. Keep recrunching the cloth until it is saturated, then start with a fresh piece.

Ragging in two colors

● As a coordinating effect for an accessory, such as the fire screen, below left, apply gray glaze and rag it off according to steps 11 to 13; then when it is dry (about 4 hours), rag on in blue glaze over the top.

IDEAS

■ Rag rolling in subtle colors makes an ideal background for stenciling. The fire screen, left, is ragged off in gray, ragged on in blue, and then decorated with a blue stenciled motif. The lines down the side are created by masking off a ⅛"-wide strip, then sponging over the top in stencil paint.

■ The pattern you get depends on the cloth—this needs to be lint-free and color-fast. A dry cloth creates a crisper pattern.

■ As with plain ragging, you can use paper bags, crunched-up paper towels or firm plastic wrap for rag rolling. All these will give a distinctly different texture.

■ For the best results, rag roll in two shades of one color, or two colors that are closely related.

Ragging and bagging are two of the easiest and quickest paint techniques to master, and the effects are amazingly versatile. Both finishes look equally good in either a traditional or a contemporary setting.

The oil-based glaze in which you do the ragging or bagging creates a light surface sheen, giving walls and other surfaces an attractive luster.

Ragging
&bagging

YOU WILL NEED:

- 2 ½ quarts base color paint (available as oil-based or acrylic-based paint)
- 2 ½ quarts oil-based glaze
- Artist's oil colors for coloring the glaze
- 1 quart paint thinner
- 4" paintbrush
- Stippling brush
- Paint roller and tray
- Paint pail
- Lint-free cotton cloth about equal to the size of a double sheet
- Small plastic bags or paper bags
- Masking tape
- Scissors
- Paper for testing

The above quantities are sufficient for a 12' x 15' room.

In this fresh, crisp-looking dining room, a background of white oil-based paint has been ragged in light green. In keeping with the wall color, the baseboards have been painted with a thin coat of green-colored glaze, allowing the background white to show through the light, horizontal-lined texture of the brushstrokes.

Ragging & bagging

These are two of the simplest of all paint techniques—and not only are they quick to do, they are cheap too. You need no specialty equipment—just pieces of lint-free cloth or a good supply of plastic bags.

Both ragging and bagging can be used on most types of walls and all manner of furniture; you might even consider using its soft, mottled texture as the background for stenciling. Although as versatile as sponging, ragging and bagging are subtractive techniques. In other words, you apply a coat of colored glaze over a plain background, and the pattern is created by

PETER TILLEY

lifting off the glaze to form a textured pattern. There are also techniques of ragging and bagging on, but these are both variations of the traditional ragging off method.

Ragging know-how

With both ragging and bagging, the effects can range from a fine, close pattern in subtle pastel on white to more dramatic and robust textures, using two different but harmonizing colors. You will find from practice or experiment that the heavier the cloth or the thicker the plastic bag, the coarser the pattern you get.

The knack with ragging or bagging is to ▶

Getting started

Preparation

● Make sure your walls are clean and dry, filling any cracks and scraping off any flaking plaster. Use a mild all-purpose household cleaner and work from the floor upward to prevent dirty streaks from forming. Rinse off the walls, if necessary, and allow surfaces to dry thoroughly, keeping the area well ventilated. To prepare wooden furniture, wash it down, then sand lightly with fine-grade sandpaper to provide a surface for the paint to adhere to.

1 Mask fixtures

● Use masking tape to protect light switches, baseboards and the angle between ceilings and walls to prevent marks from paint or glaze.

2 Apply the paint

● Apply the base coat to the walls, using a roller. Work in both diagonal directions to produce a solid, even covering of color.

3 Cutting cloth for ragging

● Make sure that the fabric you use for ragging is lint-free, clean and dry. Cut the cloth into squares the size of a large handkerchief or, if you are using old sheeting, tear the fabric into strips 16" wide, then tear each strip into squares. Prepare plenty of cut cloth to be sure you have enough to finish the project (see Equipment, left).

PHOTOGRAPHY BY ADRIAN TAYLOR

work on only a small area at a time. This way you always work on fresh, wet glaze, and always make clean imprints with the cloth or bag.

Because of this, it helps to have one person to apply the glaze and another to rag or bag off; however, one person can easily work alone in methodical patches. What is important is to start with enough of the same weight or texture of cloth or bags to complete the whole job. In both techniques you dab randomly over the surface, so it is also important to keep up an even pressure throughout your work. If you use a tightly crunched-up rag or bag, you will get a tighter "rosebud" pattern, whereas with a loosely held cloth, the ragged pattern will look more like the petals of a full-blown rose.

Colors and textures

Your color choice is limitless, but the traditional combination is to use a pastel glaze a few shades darker than the background. For a more dramatic effect, use a bright background color and an even darker glaze, such as brown over yellow, or bright green or bright blue over white. For a coordinated look, select colors that echo your upholstery fabric, curtains or carpet.

Try out different fabrics (making sure they are lint free) cut in handkerchief-sized pieces and experiment with different colors on paper to get the effect you want. When using bags, the effect is less delicate than ragging, as plastic does not absorb as much glaze as cotton. Experiment with different degrees of pressure, too. If you are too heavy-handed, you will lose the definition in the pattern, but if you dab too lightly, you will not remove enough glaze to create any texture at all. Whatever your chosen pattern, keep the same pressure throughout each project.

Ragging

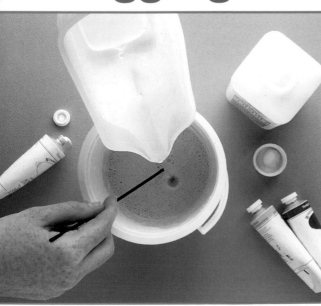

PHOTOGRAPHY BY ADRIAN TAYLOR

1 Tinting

● To color the glaze, squeeze a little artist's oil color into a small container and blend in a little paint thinner to break it up. To get the color you want, you may need to use several different colors. To lighten the color, add a touch of white; to darken it, add a little black. Pour the oil-based glaze into a paint pail, then add the colored glaze. Slowly pour in paint thinner until the glaze mixture has the consistency of light cream. Stir thoroughly to blend. It is difficult to recreate blended colors, so make sure you mix up enough to finish a whole room—at least 2 quarts.

2 Glazing

● Using a 4" brush, cover an area about 3 feet square with a thin layer of the glaze. Start in one top corner of the room and work down and across, taking care not to build up too much glaze in the corners and edges. Work the brush in both directions to spread the glaze evenly, but finish all in one direction to minimize the appearance of the brushstrokes.

HELP FILE

■ **Latex paint is too absorbent and is not suitable for this technique—it will not give you the same look. Always use the paints and glazes recommended.**

■ **If you want to add more warmth to the color of your glaze, add a dash of red or yellow. Avoid adding shades of blue, as this tends to make colors turn murky.**

■ **As you complete one wall at a time, prevent the adjoining wall from splashes by covering it up. This will also allow you to work right into the corner, too. Using one sheet of newspaper at a time, line up with the ceiling and corner and secure the paper with masking tape. Place another sheet below and secure as before. Repeat down the wall to the baseboard. Remove the masking tape before the paint dries completely; otherwise, it may stick to the wall and be difficult to remove.**

■ **If you have any paint left over, seal the can; then, making sure that the lid is firmly secured, shake the can with the bottom uppermost. This prevents a skin from forming over the surface of the paint inside.**

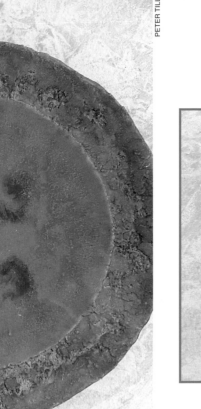

This detail shows the texture created by using a loosely scrunched-up cloth for the ragging. The effect is fresh and light, with the white background showing through enough to lighten the whole room. Use peacock-colored accessories for a really dazzling look.

As with combing or wood-graining, in which you create a pattern in a glaze by removing it from a painted background, the cloths or rags on which you wipe the glaze need to be spread out to dry where air can circulate around them. Do not leave glaze-soaked rags to dry all scrunched up—they are very combustible and could catch fire.

4 Ragging off

● While the glaze is still wet, crumple up a piece of cloth and using either one or both hands, dab over the surface while it is still tacky. Keep re-scrunching and repositioning the cloth at different angles as you work to make a random pattern, and keep using a fresh area of the cloth. When the cloth is completely saturated with glaze, start again using a fresh one. See the cautionary tip, left, for advice on drying the used rags.

5 Continuing the glazing

● Start your next square of glaze by brushing it well over the edges of the previously covered area. This ensures that there is no sign of a seam in the finished effect. Remember that you must stipple and rag while the glaze is still tacky. Depending on the temperature, it can take as little as 15 minutes for the glaze to dry. To prevent your glaze brush from drying out, either keep it immersed in the glaze or cover it lightly in plastic wrap between uses.

3 Stippling the surface

● Once you have brushed glaze over an area, take a stippling brush and use in an up-and-down pouncing motion to work out the brushstrokes. As glaze builds up on the brush, wipe it off gently on paper towels or a cloth.

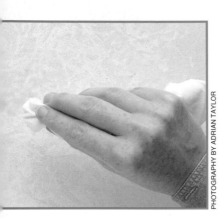

6 Spot repairs

● Where the ragging looks slightly uneven or blotchy, touch up, using a fresh piece of cloth. Work in a dabbing action, turning the cloth to even out the effect while the glaze is still wet. If the surface has dried, dab the cloth in a little of the tinted glaze, then remove the excess by dabbing on a piece of scrap paper. Work over the ragged surface, filling in any bare spots until the overall effect is even.

TIPS

If you do not have a stippling brush, you can make do with a standard paintbrush. Hold the brush with the bristles at right angles to the wall and work over the glazed surface with a dabbing motion, turning the brush as you go. Wipe off excess glaze on paper towels.

The soft textured effect in this room was achieved by bagging in a light pinky-lilac glaze over a background of white. The particular charm of ragging and bagging is that, depending on what colors you choose and the texture of rag or bag you use, you can create a look to suit any style of room. The allover texture is also ideal as a background for hanging pictures—less busy than patterned wallpaper and more interesting than a plain painted finish.

Artist's oil colors

Artist's oil colors tend to dry several shades lighter than when they are wet, so you need to bear this in mind when selecting your colors. Start by choosing the color you want from the range, then buy a slightly darker shade. When using artist's oils, always squeeze the tubes from the bottom and use sparingly—make up your chosen color, using a small spot of paint at a time. Carefully screw back the top after use to seal the tube completely. This will stop the paint from drying out and being wasted.

Bagging

1 Stippling

● Refer to the steps on pages 105 and 106 for ragging to apply the base coat and brush on the glaze. Work over the freshly glazed surface with a stippling brush, using a light dabbing action and blending the brushstrokes into the background. Clean off excess glaze from the brush by dabbing on paper towels.

TIPS

VERSATILE FINISH
Although 100% cotton is the traditional material for ragging, different fabrics, such as sacking, cotton lace, chamois leather or even a dish cloth, will give their own individual look and texture. Try using a paper bag in place of a plastic one. It will absorb the paint more than plastic, so it will give a more subtle effect. Experiment until you get the bagging effect you want.

UNEVEN WALLS
Ragging can give a face-lift to uneven plastered walls. Use bold colors, such as brown on bright yellow, to give a rustic look—this will also help to cover up any slight imperfections.

BOLD PATTERNS
Heavyweight plastic bags will create a coarse, broken pattern, quite different from that made by thin, soft plastic. Try varying the texture on panels or in an alcove to add interest to a room.

TAKING A BREAK
If for any reason you have to stop in the middle of a ragging job, always complete one entire surface—a wall or the side of a piece of furniture. When you start again, any variation in the technique will be unnoticeable.

MINIROLLERS
Small rollers, used for painting radiators, are ideal for applying the base coat to small or hard-to-reach areas.

2 **Bagging off**

● Scrunch up a plastic bag and use it to dab over the wet glaze. As with ragging, keep turning the bag at different angles as you work. As plastic is nonabsorbent, it will start to put glaze back on the wall when it is covered, so keep changing to a clean bag. Work with an even pressure all over.

3 **Touching up**

● Stand back from your work to check it. If there are uneven patches, load a brush with a little glaze, and with a plastic bag in the other hand, cover over the bare patch and use the bag to dab it off in an even pattern.

4 **Finishing touch**

● Before removing the masking tape, work along the edge of the decorated wall with a paintbrush loaded with a little glaze to fill in any bare spots.

Transform a set of matching storage jars with bagging in just three colors. The contrasting colors are used in different combinations for a harmonizing effect. The jar on the left was given a base coat of tangerine paint; the center one, green; and the one on the right, yellow. Then, in sequence, the jars were ragged in yellow, tangerine and green. Spray varnish for a wipe-clean finish and swap the lids between the jars for a fun effect.

This plain kitchen chair takes on a new look when given the ragging treatment. To keep the pattern in proportion to the chair, a tightly scrunched light-weight plastic bag was used to create the small random "rosebud" pattern.

Color guide

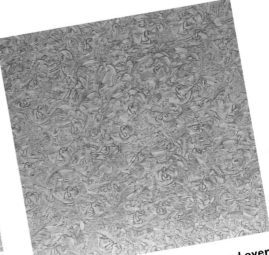

● A coral glaze has been ragged over a soft peach base to give a tone-on-tone effect for a traditional look.

● Here, peach glaze has been used over orange, using the bagging technique, to give an extra depth of color.

● A rich rose pink glaze was bagged over a base of soft peach—the two colors give a harmonious shading together.

● Ragging in gray over mauve gives a softly defined look to the technique and creates a look of crushed velvet.

● Bag one shade of yellow over another for a gentle texture. Oatmeal over a paler yellow base gives a traditional look.

● Using a soft green glaze over a sand-colored base shows up the crisp texture of the bagging pattern.

● Choose tone-on-tone combinations, such as cornflower blue over pale blue, to show the classic crunchy texture.

● Use a pale aqua-colored glaze over a darker aqua base coat for a light cloudy look on a bagged finish.

● For a cool sophisticated look, choose a gray glaze and bag it over a background of white.

Design ideas

Choose colors and textures to create just the mood you want for any room. Projects can vary from pieces of furniture to accessories or whole walls. Ragging and bagging add definition and interest to any plain surface.

ABODE UK

Classic style in a bathroom

▲ This unusual bathroom combines several paint effects, including marbling on the wall above the bathtub and on the tub panel—but the basin wall shows off a subtle ragged effect perfectly. A light ocher-colored glaze has been ragged over a sandy background to give a look not unlike walnut. This mottled two-tone effect makes a soft background for a border of stenciled wreaths in brown and ocher near the ceiling. The room successfully combines classical elegance and oriental glamour.

Pastel shades

◀ The simple elegance of this gently colored living room is enhanced by a very soft ragging of apricot over cream. To get a really soft effect, use thin, lightweight cotton. This will absorb a lot of glaze and create a very delicate texture.

Clever disguise

▶Although the wall above the radiator has ridged paneling, the effect of crisply textured ragging distracts the eye and draws the attention away from the shadows and ridges. Use a heavy weight of cloth (or a firm plastic bag) to give a scrunchy and very distinct texture on uneven wall surfaces to give an impression of evenness.

Rustic cupboard

◀ Ragging or bagging are ideal for giving a face-lift to tired pieces of furniture and junk-shop finds. This two-door paneled cupboard has been ragged in a rich chestnut glaze over a light tan background, and the effect is almost woodlike. Use rustic colors together, as here, to make furniture fit in with a fresh country look—or select colors from your curtains, wallpaper or upholstery to rag or bag small items of furniture to give an individual, accessorized look.

Rich reds

▶ A glaze of brick red over a softer red base lends a regal look to this entrance hall. To add to the impression of space, the inside of the door on the far right has been ragged in the same way as the walls and blends into the background. Use a ragged or bagged texture to break up large expanses of wall that would otherwise look dull if painted in an allover color. Because of the natural shine to the glaze, rich colors look even richer when given the ragging treatment.

Color-washing

This alternative color-washing technique uses acrylic glazing liquid as a base for your color, so you can create a whole range of subtle, textured effects.

Color-washing is an attractive technique for plain walls, and when it comes to shades and colorways, the possibilities are endless. You don't need much in the way of equipment—just a sponge and a paintbrush.

The basic technique uses latex paint diluted with water to make a thin wash. Effective and quick-drying, this wash adds interest to plain, matte walls. For a textured look, however, you need a thicker base for your color. So, flat latex paint is mixed with an acrylic glaze. The glaze medium prolongs the drying time, so you can create more complex and controlled patterns.

The technique

Above the faux chair rail, peach glaze, followed by a wash of cream, has been applied in a series of zigzag strokes to create a crosshatch effect. Below the chair rail, dark brown, peach and cream have been combined, washed one on top of the other for a subtle buildup of color.

The chair rail itself is created with masking tape and decorated with the basic color-washing technique, using a textured sponge, to give a soft, mottled look.

YOU WILL NEED:
- 1 quart flat latex paint in dark brown, cream and peach
- 1 to 2 quarts acrylic glaze
- Medium-sized paintbrush
- Two large paintbrushes
- Sponge
- Two paint pails
- Mixing sticks
- Measuring cup
- Tape measure
- Pencil
- 1"-wide masking tape
- ½"-wide masking tape
- Scissors
- Plastic drop cloth
- Plain paper
- Ruler

1 Mark the chair rail line

● Measure 44" up from your baseboard, marking points at regular intervals along the wall. Then mask a line above these pencil marks, using the 1"-wide masking tape. This will serve as a marker for the upper limit of your faux chair rail.

2 Paint the lower wall

● Apply the first coat of dark brown flat latex paint below the masking tape. Let dry for up to 4 hours, then apply a second coat to give a solid layer of color. Allow a further 4 hours for the paint to dry thoroughly.

3 Prepare the sponge

● Cut the sponge in half (setting aside half for later use) and texture the surface, picking out lumps to create a rough effect. Pull out sections from the edges, too, so that there are no hard corners. (The sponge will be used for the faux chair rail.)

4 Mix the glaze and latex paint

● Pour some acrylic glaze into each of the paint pails. Add a small amount of cream latex to one pail and some peach to the other. Stir well, adding water until the consistency is like milk.

5 Mask the paintwork

● Remove masking tape along the rail line and remask, this time moving the tape below the pencil marks to protect the brown paintwork. For extra protection, tape a plastic drop cloth over the newly painted section.

6 Apply the peach glaze

● Using the medium-sized paintbrush, apply the peach glaze to the wall above the masking tape. Work across the wall in vertical sections. Move down each section, using short, overlapping zigzag strokes to build up a textured, crosshatch design. Allow to dry for 2–3 hours.

7 Apply the cream glaze

● Using a large paintbrush, apply the cream glaze in the same way as step 6, this time using long, sweeping strokes.

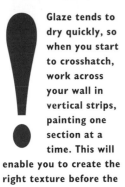

8 Spread the cream glaze

● While the glaze is still wet, use a clean large paintbrush to spread it as thinly as you can. When you are satisfied with the texture, allow to dry.

! Glaze tends to dry quickly, so when you start to crosshatch, work across your wall in vertical strips, painting one section at a time. This will enable you to create the right texture before the glaze hardens.

9 Mark the chair rail base

● Measure 4¾" down from the top of the masking tape and make regular pencil marks along the wall. Then mask off above the pencil marks with the 1"-wide masking tape.

10 Apply the peach glaze

● Apply the peach glaze below the second line of masking tape with a medium-sized paintbrush, using long, random strokes.

TIPS

■ When spreading the glaze, work as quickly and roughly as you like. Any unevenness adds to the overall texture.

■ Pale colors work best on a white or an off-white base color. For a stronger or more sophisticated color-wash, use a dark base with other strong tones on top.

■ A color-washed wall provides an ideal backdrop for stenciling. Here, the lattice rail frames a stenciled leaf motif.

■ Use flat or gloss varnish over the color-wash to give extra protection. The flat will give a whitewash feel, suitable for pale country-style walls. The gloss will give a mock lacquer look, which is ideal with rich or dark colors.

■ The technique of color-washing combines well with other paint effects. Try a paint scheme that uses color-wash above the chair rail and stippling or sponging below.

11 Texture the peach glaze

● With the untextured sponge half, work across the wet glaze in short, random strokes. The edges that the sponge creates will add to the texture. Allow to dry for 2–3 hours. Wash the sponge thoroughly after use.

12 Apply cream glaze

● Dip the washed sponge into the cream glaze and apply to the wall in short, random strokes. Build on the angular pattern, working lightly so that the colors beneath still show through. Allow to dry for 2 hours.

13 Mask within the chair rail line

● Remove all masking tape; then tape ½"-wide masking tape above and below the color-washed surfaces inside the brown chair rail stripe. To protect the color-washed walls, tape paper to the outside of both rows of masking tape.

14 Mark the tape

● With ruler and pencil, measure along both strips of masking tape, making pencil marks every 2½". Make sure both sets of pencil marks align with each other.

15 Mask off lattice design

● Using the ½"-wide masking tape, connect every second pencil mark to create diagonal stripes. Repeat with the tape running in the opposite direction to complete a lattice.

HELP FILE

■ Small mistakes are unlikely to be visible from a distance and can add to the overall feel of texture. Large, noticeable errors (such as color-wash bleeding into the solid brown rail areas) can be touched up when you have finished.

16 Color-wash the lattice

● With the textured sponge half, lightly color-wash the cream glaze over the masked area. Wipe over the masking tape as lightly as possible to minimize bleeding. Allow to dry for 2 hours.

17 Double the lattice

● Now create a series of smaller diamonds with the ½"-wide masking tape, pressing each diagonal strip down firmly to prevent your final coat from bleeding beneath.

18 Repeat color-washing

● Repeat the cream color-washing with the textured sponge. Build up several thin coats to achieve a color difference between the two color-washed layers.

19 Touching up

● When finished, remove all the masking tape, touch up any faint bleeding on the brown base color, then allow to dry for at least 4 hours.

Color guide

● Color-wash with cool green over flat latex paint for a chalky effect that is coarse and rustic.

● Use a soft, pale lilac, and work in slightly curved strokes to create a soft, cloudy effect over a base of satin latex paint.

● Give a chunky, rustic look with a color-wash of ocher over cream, allowing the brushstrokes to show.

● Color-wash in two colors—light orange and peach—over cream for a warm, cloudy effect.

● Wash light turquoise blue over a white background to give an unusual sky effect to a ceiling, or use for a bathroom.

● Create a rustic look with a warm, earthy brown, ideal for a kitchen or breakfast nook.

● Use misty mauve in swirls for a romantic bedroom. Make a feature of the brushstrokes as you gain experience.

● Create patches of color in dull orange, then color-wash over the top in a mixture of the base color and orange.

● Use a busy textured effect such as this in small areas—in an alcove, behind shelves or in a panel.

DESIGN ideas

Color-wash can be as bright or subtle, as textured or as cloudy as you like, and the effect is always more charming and easy on the eye than a plain color, as these different rooms show.

A formal living room with framed pictures, an elegant gilded mirror and a marble fireplace is softened by color-washing in bright pea green. A very soft effect like this, where the brushstrokes are scarcely visible, is achieved by softening the color-washing all over with a damp brush or by rubbing in patches with a barely damp sponge. ▶

◀ Color-washing in emerald green over white breaks up a plain wall in a traditional Victorian-style bathroom. A green this bright, if used as a solid wall color, would be overpowering, but the texture of color-washing allows you to use vibrant colors over very large areas.

ELIZABETH WHITING ASSOCIATES

▲ Ocher is a favorite shade for color-washing, and the effects can vary from rustic to sophisticated, as in the corner, above. Color-washed walls, with their soft, translucent shading, look particularly good as a background to natural wood. With untreated oak or pine, the effect is cottagey and naive, whereas with polished and shining wood, the effect has a touch of elegance.

▲ Dazzling color-washed mauve combined with stark white and shining red give a sparsely furnished bedroom a touch of the exotic Orient. If you find such bright colors uncomfortable in a bedroom, tone down the mauve with white for a softer, more romantic look and add accessories in pinks or dull purply blues.

◄ A thin color-washing of a rich reddish color makes a good background for displaying pictures and gives color and texture without regular patterns to distract the eye. Try color-washing as the background to shelves, or behind a collection of wall-mounted plates for a charming, rustic effect.

▲ By clever use of masking tape you can decorate a room with soft, color-washed stripes. Mask off one measured stripe with a vertical line of tape and color-wash up to it in one color. When this has dried, reposition the tape so that it masks the first stripe of color-washing. Continue around the room in measured stripes, calculating the width so that you finish with a complete stripe at the corners. In this room, gray-blue and yellow make a pretty and fresh contrast of light and dark in a softly colored bedroom.

Brick & Sands

Give plain walls a classy, fashionable finish with two ingenious faux effects that create the illusion of naturally aged stonework.

Choose either brick, aged by the passage of time—warm, mellow reds and a bold, rough surface; or sandstone, with its soft, subtle colors and cool elegance capturing centuries in its smooth, mottled texture. Faux stonework has a decorative style all its own. Far from looking stark or unfinished, the look is comfortable yet sophisticated, and both techniques are good cosmetic treatments for less-than-perfect walls.

Stripping walls back to bare brick or stone is expensive and labor-intensive, but with these easy-to-follow techniques you need only simple, inexpensive materials to transform walls and accessories. So whichever look you recreate—the gentle, natural feel of sandstone or the dramatic, eye-catching texture of brick—take the quick and easy option with these clever faux effects, which recreate the look without the expense.

tone

Sandstone bedroom

Create a beautiful, romantic bedroom fit for a fairy-tale castle, using this deceptively simple faux effect.

PHOTOGRAPHY BY LIZZIE ORME

EQUIPMENT

YOU WILL NEED:
- Plaster molding
- 4 quarts satin-finish oil-based paint in cream
- Artist's oil colors in burnt sienna, burnt umber and pale ocher
- Paint thinner
- Paintbrush
- Lining brush
- Two synthetic sponges
- Plumb line
- Tape measure
- Pencil
- Saw
- Miter box
- Nails
- Hammer
- Adhesive
- Two mixing bowls
- Mixing sticks
- Ruler

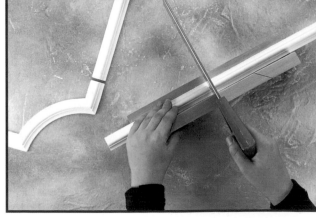

1 Attach molding

● Using the plumb line, tape measure and pencil, mark the shape and position of the trimmed panels on the walls. Using the saw and miter box, cut the molding to size, then attach to the wall with nails or an appropriate adhesive

126

3 Mix glaze

● In a bowl, mix burnt sienna, burnt umber and pale ocher artist's oil colors with paint thinner to make a light terra-cotta, stirring well until the consistency is like thin cream.

4 Rub on glaze

● Cut one sponge in half and load with terra-cotta glaze. Using large, random circular movements, rub the glaze over the surface of the wall, making sure that you cover the crevices of the molding with glaze.

5 Rub off

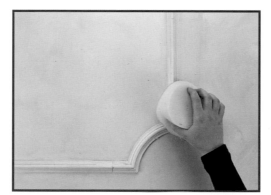

● Wait 5 minutes for the glaze to start to dry; then, using the other half of the sponge, rub over the wall with a random circular motion. The aim is to soften and blend the texture by removing some of the glaze.

6 Mark out a grid

● Using the plumb line, draw horizontal lines 10¼" apart down the wall. Divide these with a vertical line every 18", starting 9" in from the left on alternate lines, to give a block effect.

2 Apply the cream base

● Paint the walls, including the attached molding and the chair rail, with an even coat of the cream paint. Let dry 12–16 hours; apply a second coat if the coverage is not solid enough.

7 Paint over pencil lines

● In a bowl, mix burnt umber and a little pale ocher artist's oils with paint thinner. Load the lining brush with this glaze and, using long, even strokes, paint over the pencil lines.

TIPS

■ If you are working in a large room, apply the terra-cotta glaze to one wall at a time, rubbing it back before going on to the other walls. If you cover too large an area, the glaze may dry before you have a chance to soften it. If possible, work with a second person— one applying the glaze, the other following 5 minutes behind, rubbing it back.

■ If either of the glazes dries before you soften it, dampen a sponge with a little paint thinner and rub it lightly over the affected area.

■ If the glazes disappear when you rub them back, they are still too wet. Apply more glaze to the affected area and wait 5–10 minutes before continuing.

■ Be sparing with the number of cracks you paint on; if you overdo it, you will spoil the overall effect. Limit the number to five or six for a 12' x 15' room.

■ For a realistic finish, position the cracks around the molding or the chair rail, as these are the places where cracks are most likely to develop.

127

8 Soften the lines

● Wait 5 minutes; then work along each line with a clean sponge, gently blurring the glaze. Try not to over-blur the corners—they need to be distinct.

9 Add realistic cracks

● Load the lining brush with the dark glaze and, in a few chosen spots, paint a narrow crack that starts on a blurred line and stretches toward the middle of a stone. After 5 minutes, blur gently with a clean, dry sponge.

Brick hall and stairwell

Turn an unimaginative hallway into an entrance with real impact. This quick-drying effect uses flat latex paint, spray paints and sand, combined with a little imagination.

YOU WILL NEED:

- 3 quarts satin-finish latex paint in beige
- 3–4 quarts flat latex paint in brick red
- Spray paints in chestnut brown and beige
- 2 lbs sand
- Small paintbrush
- Medium-sized paintbrush
- Tape measure
- Ruler
- Pencil
- Plumb line
- ½"-wide masking tape
- Scissors
- Two paint pails
- Mixing sticks
- Hair dryer

EQUIPMENT

1 Apply base color

● Clean the walls thoroughly to ensure that they are free from grease. When dry, apply an even coat of beige satin-finish latex paint, then allow to dry for 2–4 hours. If necessary, add a second coat.

2 Measure and mask off brick grid

● Draw horizontal pencil lines at 3" intervals down the wall. Divide these horizontal bands with a vertical line every 8½", starting the measurements 4¼" in from the left on every other line, to give a brick effect. Center strips of masking tape over the pencil lines.

3 Mix paint

● In a paint pail, mix the brick red flat latex paint with about half as much sand. Add the sand slowly, stirring thoroughly to distribute it through the paint. Continue to add sand until the mixture is quite stiff, forming soft peaks as you stir it.

! When you apply the red paint mixture, do not paint over the masking tape. If you do, it will be impossible to remove the tape without pulling off lumps of the paint mixture, thus spoiling the overall effect. Try to stay within the tape as much as possible.

4 Paint the bricks

● Using the small paintbrush and working on one brick at a time, apply the paint mixture as thickly as possible, using short, dabbing brushstrokes. Repeat on 4 or 5 bricks, then use the hair dryer to seal the surface and shorten the drying time (see Tips, page 131). Repeat the process until you have covered all the bricks.

5 Remove tape

● Once the surface of the bricks is dry, remove the masking tape, gently easing the tape out from under the edge of each brick. Take care not to pull the paint mixture off the wall with the tape. Let the wall dry completely before continuing.

6 Paint in mortar lines

● In a paint pail, mix some beige latex paint with sand until the consistency is stiff. Using a finger or a large artist's brush, apply around the bricks to imitate mortar. Let dry 2 hours.

7 Spray with brown and beige paints

● Standing at least 3' back from the wall and pointing the spray can slightly upward, spray the bricks randomly with the chestnut brown color, trying to concentrate the color more on one side of the bricks to indicate shadow. When the paint is dry, repeat with the beige spray paint, using the color to break up any expanse of dark brown or red, and to add a cloudiness to the texture.

TIPS

■ The setting you use on the hair dryer will affect the way the brickwork looks. If you use the lowest setting, the texture of the paint will be unaffected but the drying time will be shortened. If you use a medium setting, the air current may shift the paint around, creating a smoother texture. On the highest setting, if you hold the hair dryer close to the surface, the paint mixture may crack, creating an aged and worn appearance.

■ If you leave the red or beige paint mixtures to stand and they become unworkable, add a little water until the mixture regains the right consistency.

Design ideas

■ The soft, pale elegance of sandstone is the perfect finish for small pieces of furniture and accessories, such as this striking lamp base, right. Whatever you are decorating, the technique stays the same—just adapt the size of the blocks and cracks to suit the item you are working on. And since real sandstone comes in many different tones—from a warm, creamy terra-cotta to a pale, cold gray—you need only change the artist's oil colors you use to create a totally new look for this effect. The lamp base, which has a ceramic surface, was coated with all-purpose primer before applying the base color of pale cream oil-based paint. Then burnt umber artist's oil color was diluted with paint thinner to make a very thin wash, which was heavily rubbed back with a clean sponge to give a cooler and grayer tone to the sandstone. If you omit the mortar lines, you instantly create the illusion of a lamp base cut from one piece of real sandstone. For a realistic finish, limit the number of cracks on a small item; on something as small as this lamp base, one large crack is sufficient.

Use this technique to add weight and age to pieces of plaster architecture, such as pillars and pedestals—the effect is classy and sophisticated and very convincing.

■ You do not need to limit the brick technique to flat, smooth surfaces. The eye-catching trunk, below, was transformed using soft, neutral colors for the bricks. To create this subtle look, use soft beiges and browns for the base and top coats. You can vary the texture to suit the colors you choose; the less sand you add to the paint, the smoother the bricks will be.

To age the bricks, apply cream and chestnut brown spray paints, adding a touch of black to create an extra sense of depth. Although the sand mixture forms a durable surface, you can protect accessories that are likely to suffer a lot of wear and tear with a coat of water-based matte varnish.

Dragging

A traditional glaze technique for flat surfaces, dragging with a brush gives an elegant, two-color grained texture – perfect for walls, doors and furniture.

Although it is traditional to use related colors for the base coat and the dragging, this cabinet shows how effective unrelated colors can be. When combining colors such as the pink and green used here, avoid using strong contrasts of tone which might jar and instead choose similar shades that sit comfortably together.

Pick out the detailing of a paneled cabinet with dragging in different colors. Here we have selected just one base color and two complementary pastel tones for coloring the glaze. Following the steps on pages 135-137, the whole cabinet was primed and painted in a soft pale green. Then, the panel and surround were dragged in pink glaze, and the rest of the cabinet was dragged in a darker green.

EQUIPMENT

YOU WILL NEED:
- I quart matte-finish oil-based paint in base color
- I quart oil-based glaze
- Artist's oil colors to tint the glaze
- Paint thinner
- 3"-wide paintbrush
- I"-wide paintbrush
- 3"-wide dragging brush
- Medium-grade sandpaper
- Fine-grade sandpaper
- Cloth or paper towels

Dragging was traditionally an eighteenth-century decoration for woodwork and doors. Then, in the 1930s, dragging grew popular again as a way to imitate the natural grain of wood. Now it is fashionable, along with sponging, bagging and many other decorative paint effects, as a finish in its own right, giving an elegant and textured two-tone look.

Dragging know-how

As a technique, dragging is similar to other subtractive glaze effects: You paint a background of matte-finish oil-based paint over the prepared surface, then brush a glaze tinted in a contrasting color over the dry base coat. You then remove the glaze in straight, unbroken lines to leave a pattern with the base color showing through. As with other techniques such as wood-graining or combing, you need a particular tool to create the effect; for dragging you need a dragging brush.

This brush is thinner in depth and has longer bristles than the average paintbrush—about 4" on average—and these bristles have a mixture of different textures, varying from very fine to very coarse. It is this variation in texture that produces the characteristic dragged look: As you drag the bristles down the glaze, the coarser bristles press between the softer ones, removing the glaze more heavily and creating straight lines.

Dragging brushes are available in a range of widths. If you only buy one, choose a 3"-wide brush, which will be adaptable for most projects. (Although you can get a similar look with a paintbrush, the effect will be much less defined.)

Color and effects

Whether you are dragging on a small piece of furniture or on walls, it is important to get the right balance between the base color and the glaze. Traditionally, the base is lighter than the glaze, and the most harmonious effects come from selecting shades which are adjacent on ▶

1 Prepare the surface

● Wipe the door clean with an all-purpose cleaner or mild household detergent. Using medium-grade sandpaper, rub down the surface to remove any loose or blistered paint. Dust off with a clean brush or cloth and repeat, using fine-grade sandpaper for a smooth finish. Brush off as before, then wipe with a damp cloth and allow to dry.

PHOTOGRAPHY BY ADRIAN TAYLOR

Front door

● This paneled front door was painted with a pink base coat, then a deep red glaze was dragged over the top, working in the order as shown in the Help File, page 137. A final coat of oil-based varnish gives the door a robust finish to stand up to wear and weather.

PETER TILLEY

2 Prime the surface

● Apply a primer suitable for wood surfaces, working it well into the wood in the direction of the grain of each part of the door. One coat of primer will be sufficient on a painted surface, but for a really solid base over bare wood, apply a second coat of primer when the first coat has dried. An oil-based primer will take about 6 hours to be dry enough to recoat.

3 Apply the base coat

● Apply a base of oil-based paint to the surface of the door, using a 3"-wide brush. Finish, or lay off, the paint with brushstrokes in the direction of the wood grain—this is the direction in which you will be dragging. The surface should have a smooth, flat finish with no visible brushstrokes.

TIPS

MIXING GLAZE

If you need only a small amount of glaze, pour the correct quantity of oil-based glaze into a screw-top jar and add a little artist's oil color and a little paint thinner. Shake well to blend, adding more oil color to make the color you want. When the glaze is well mixed, stir in enough paint thinner to make the consistency you need and to disperse any bubbles in the glaze.

DRAGGING A WALL

Although it is tricky to drag a whole wall, it is possible. Use a ladder and work down from the top, making sure that you do not stop the brush while it is in contact with the wall, as this will make a hard break. When you can no longer reach to drag the brush downward, gradually lift the brush away, still dragging downward. Move down the ladder; then, to start the rest of the stroke, begin the downward movement before the brush makes contact with the wall. Make sure that you do not stop at the same level every time but alternate to make the break less visible.

135

the color wheel (see Color Know-how, page 5). However, there are no hard-and-fast rules—experiment to get unusual and attractive effects.

It is worth practicing before you start a project. Paint a piece of sealed wood or cardboard in your chosen background color, allow it to dry, then test different colors of glaze over it. This is a good opportunity to perfect your technique.

Dragging ideas

The even grain of dragging combines well with other techniques. Try a dragged surround to a door where the panels are sponged, ragged, woodgrained or stippled. Another idea is to work a two-technique effect above and below a chair rail. By dividing a wall horizontally and dragging only below the rail, you reduce the length of each dragged stroke, making it easier to work in perfect lines without pausing or shaking.

Getting started

Always work on a properly prepared surface; a little extra time spent ensuring that your door, wall or piece of furniture is smooth, clean and dust-free is well worth while. Make sure that the surface for dragging is smooth by sanding it with fine-grade sandpaper; then, if you are working on a porous surface, such as untreated wood, apply an appropriate primer to seal it. Use only oil-based primer if you are going to use traditional oil-based paint as a base. If you use satin-finish acrylic paint, use a water-based primer; you can then use an oil-based glaze over the acrylic base.

Tricks for even dragging

Try to restrict yourself to a dragged drop that is no longer than your reach, so do not attempt to drag a whole wall, especially not as a first project. Instead, work on an area below a chair rail or in an alcove. To keep your lines straight, use a plumb line on wide areas of dragging, repositioning it with reusable adhesive as you go. For a neat finish, wipe away any splashes of glaze or smudged edges with a clean cloth while the glaze is still wet. Just follow the steps and you can be sure of a neat and professional finish. Remember, as with any glaze technique, you can always wipe away an error and start again.

PHOTOGRAPHY BY ADRIAN TAYLOR

4 Tint the glaze

● Squeeze a dab of oil color into a small container and pour in a little paint thinner. Mix well to disperse the oil color, then pour into the glaze in a paint pail, stirring well. Add paint thinner until the glaze has the consistency of thin cream.

6 Loading the brush

● Dip the dragging brush into the glaze to within about ¾" of the top. Pull the brush between your index and middle fingers to press excess glaze back into the paint can. Wipe your fingers on a cloth dampened with paint thinner.

5 Apply the glaze

● Apply the glaze one area at a time, following the order of work in the Help File, opposite. Spread the glaze evenly and lay off each area in the direction of the grain of the wood beneath it. On paneled doors the grain runs vertically, except for the top, bottom and center horizontal rails.

7 Dragging

● Place the dragging brush at the top left corner of the panel so that the bristles just overlap the top. Holding the brush at about a 30-degree angle to the door, pull it down in line with the left edge. Exert enough pressure for the bristles to flex in the middle. Wipe the excess glaze from the brush frequently on paper towels.

Drag a window-box in colors to match your front door. This too will need to be varnished as protection against the weather.

PETER TILLEY

8 Cleaning up

● While the glaze is still wet, dampen a cloth with a little paint thinner and use to wipe away any smudged edges or areas where glaze has spattered. This should be easy to remove, provided it has not started to dry. Protect an outside door with one or two coats of varnish.

It is important to work each new dragged stroke next to a wet edge. If you stop work with an area glazed but undragged, and let it dry, then try to apply wet glaze over the top, you will get an uneven depth of color. Always complete a definite area—a wall, a panel, one side of a piece of furniture or the top of a table—before taking a break.

Although the glaze itself is sufficient protection for indoor dragging, you will need to give a coat of varnish to the outside of a door against wear and tear.

PETER TILLEY

DRAGGING A PANELED DOOR
If you can, take the door off its hinges and lay it flat. Remove the handle

and prepare and paint as on page 135, then glaze and drag in the following order: 1. The panels and their molding, working the sides vertically and the top and bottom horizontally. 2. Drag the center stiles vertically. 3. Drag the top, bottom and center rails horizontally. 4. Drag the outer stiles vertically, working over both side edges of the horizontal rails. 5. Drag the top of the architrave horizontally. 6. Drag the sides of the architrave vertically. Replace the door handle when dry.

Filling in a panel

After filling in the center panel, work the surrounding molding using a small paintbrush as a dragging brush. Work in lines parallel to the panel. Fill in the top and bottom molding by dragging the brush through the glaze horizontally, as illustrated below.

SURFACES
The surface for dragging must be smooth and flat. A good plaster finish, sheetrock, lining paper, fine cork tiling, glass, good wood furniture, laminates and metal are ideal. Curved walls, rough plastering, textured wallpaper, stone, brick and floorboards are not suitable.

Color guide

● **Create a subtle color effect by using a light cream base coat with a purple glaze dragged over the top.**

● **Highlight a lighter green base coat with a darker glaze color. Tone-on-tone colors are a traditional combination.**

● **Choose a dark pink to go over a pale gray base coat to create a gentle, sophisticated eighteenth-century look.**

● **Imitate a 1930's look by using a pale blue glaze over a warm yellow base coat.**

● **Drag a bright red glaze over a paler pink to give a rich and distinctive depth of color.**

● **Apply a white glaze and drag it over a pastel blue base coat for a crisp, fresh texture.**

● **Work burnt orange glaze over a cream base coat to imitate the grain found in natural woods.**

● **For a striking effect, drag a bright red glaze over a pale blue base coat. The combination creates a purplish glow.**

● **Combine closely related colors, such as an aqua glaze over a dark blue base, to give a subtle, textured finish.**

Dragging
small items

Book shelf

To give a face-lift to a plain painted wood bookshelf, use a rich creamy yellow base coat over the whole unit. Once this coat is dry, apply a leaf green glaze on the outside only and drag in the direction of the grain. Glaze the front edges of the shelves and the base, then drag horizontally.

Trinket box

Drag a small box in colors to give a look of tropical hardwood. Make sure your box is free from grease and dust, then cover with a base coat of deep brown. Drag over the top in a rich orange glaze for an effect that closely resembles the grain of wood.

Breakfast tray

Use a new wooden tray or prepare the surface of an old one by cleaning and sanding. Paint all over in white, then drag in bright yellow, keeping the strokes going down the length of the tray on the flat surface and long sides and across the tray at the short ends. Coat with varnish to give added protection against wear.

HELP FILE

■ "Curtaining" is one of the most common problems with dragging. This is a thick blobby effect, most likely to happen at the top of a dragged surface, where the brush takes a grip on the glaze. To avoid this, apply the glaze sparingly at the very top of any surface for dragging. To correct curtaining, take a dry paintbrush and tease the glaze downward in the direction of the dragging. If your dragging is beyond help, wipe it away with a cloth moistened with paint thinner, brush over fresh glaze and start again.

■ Because you pick up glaze on the brush as you drag, the bottom end of a long dragged strip may become heavy with glaze. To avoid this, ease the pressure on the brush slightly at the end of the stroke so that the area of the bristles that picks up the glaze is slightly nearer the end of the brush and less saturated with glaze than the middle of the bristles.

DESIGN ideas

The effects from dragging can be as bright or as subtle as you choose. It is a versatile technique which combines well with other paint effects, such as bagging, sponging and color-washing, and even makes a good background to show off stenciling.

ALL PHOTOGRAPHS ELIZABETH WHITING

▶ In this kitchen dragging in a gray-blue glaze over a white background has been used to link the cabinets, the door and the backs of the shelves. With its gentle lined texture, dragging goes well with other paint techniques, such as the yellow color-washing on the walls, giving a look which is softer than solid color.

◀ Clever use of paint techniques and *trompe l'oeil* paneling effects are set against a striped wallpaper in matching colors to give this hallway a formal elegance. In the area below the chair rail, dragging in honey yellow over cream has been used to give the impression of wood trim around false marble paneling.

▼ Very subtle dragging in pink over pale pink gives a soft look that makes a perfect background for stenciling. For a dragged effect as subtle as this, you could doctor an ordinary paintbrush. Snip out clusters of bristles so that the brush creates dragged lines when you pull it through the glaze.

Uneven walls

Damaged or uneven walls need not be a problem or restrict the way you decorate them. Whether you have cracked walls you need to cover or textured finishes you want to disguise, there is a quick and affordable solution—and a paint technique to add an individual touch.

Uneven wall problems come in many forms—you may have damaged plaster that needs strengthening and concealing, or perhaps you have a paintable wallcovering, such as Anaglypta wallpaper, that is bolstering up crumbly plaster. In either case, replastering would be expensive. But there is no need to replaster—there are solutions and ideas for all types of uneven or damaged walls. New textured paints and plasters, applied by brush, roller or float, open up a range of possibilities with finishes that will cover all manner of wall problems. Whatever the surface, there are ways to add a touch of originality.

Cover-up treatments

If you have damaged plaster walls and you do not want to replaster, the answer is a textured finish that will fill and reinforce the damaged surface and make ready the wall for a more imaginative decoration. Ideal for this are treatments such as impasto, ready-mixed plaster and textured paint; all of these can be given a random or a patterned finish to suit a variety of different paint techniques.

Textured walls

An existing textured finish can be treated in a number of ways to give unusual and striking effects. You can even apply impasto over a sound covering of a paintable wallcovering; it saves stripping the walls and gives a whole new appearance. Similarly, applied plaster finishes, either with a random or a patterned texture, are an ideal base for a variety of different paint effects. Simply select a treatment and a paint finish to suit your walls and the look you want to create.

Ways with plaster

One of the best ways of disguising and enhancing bare or scarred plaster walls is to apply a color-wash over a base color. Fill any cracks or holes with an all-purpose filler, then prime the filler with diluted latex paint. Apply a base of flat latex paint in a light color and color-wash, as in the steps below. These walls were painted white with a ready-to-use color-wash in terra-cotta over the top.

Preparation

● Before you apply any kind of paint to bare, untreated plaster, seal it with a primer (see Tips, opposite). This will prevent the first coat of paint from sinking into the plaster and provides a good base for painting.

1 Apply base coat

● Paint the primed walls with flat latex paint in cream or white, using a large paintbrush or a roller. Allow 2–4 hours for the paint to dry completely.

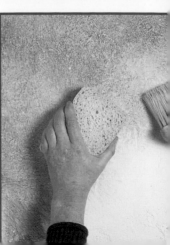

Impasto

Impasto is a thick, cream-colored base that dries to an attractive plaster finish, ideal for covering imperfect walls. Spread it roughly with a spatula for a dramatic textured effect, or apply it with a paintbrush as a background for different paint techniques.

1 Disguising cracks

● Clean out any loose plaster from the cracks and wipe the surface clean. Apply the impasto as thickly as you want, working it into the cracks and finishing it with random brushstrokes. Allow about 2 hours to dry completely.

● For a richly colored finish, apply a ready-to-use color-wash in a dark color, such as mulberry. Use a household sponge to spread the wash thickly in wide sweeps, as in the steps, below left. Allow about 2 hours to dry. This makes an ideal textured background for stenciling.

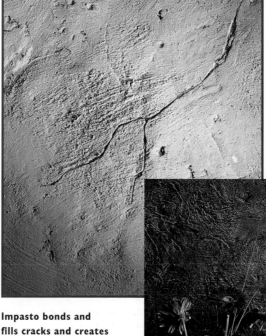

Impasto bonds and fills cracks and creates a perfect finish for paint techniques.

2 Apply color-wash

● Pick up ready-to-use color-wash on a household sponge and spread the wash over the wall in wide diagonal sweeps, covering about 3 square feet at a time. Hold a hog-hair brush in your other hand and use it to soften the overlap lines as you work.

TIPS

PRIMERS
You can use several different mediums for sealing and priming plaster. As a good base for latex paint, mix water and the base color paint in a ratio of 4 to 1, and brush the mixture over the plaster. Or you can use white glue (a water-based glue) diluted in the same ratio to give a clear, shiny surface. Otherwise, brush with sand-and-seal shellac, a denatured alcohol-based sealant, in the same way.

MASKING
When color-washing, save time masking off windows and doors with tape by painting a border of color-wash around the window and the door frames and along the top of the baseboards. Use a clean cloth to wipe away any blotches of color-wash that splash on the paintwork while it is still wet. Then wipe lightly over the still-wet lines with a household sponge. This gives a soft outline in which to work when you start to apply color-wash over the main wall area.

RUSTIC AGING
Recreate the look of old Tuscan walls by rubbing down the color-washed plaster when dry, using fine-grade sandpaper for a mellow and weathered appearance.

143

Rough plaster

Color-washing is an ideal technique to use over rough plaster, giving depths of translucent color and emphasizing the broken texture of the wall. If the plaster is bare, seal it with primer (see Tips, page 143, then paint with white flat latex paint. Work a dark blue, ready-to-use color-wash into the surface, using a sponge or a brush, and softening as you work with a badger-hair softener.

Coarse plaster

● To color-wash over very uneven plaster, use a hog-hair brush to work the color into the textured surface. Load the brush with plenty of glaze and brush in upward diagonal strokes, pressing the brush into the contours of the plaster to give an allover cover. The base should show through slightly over the raised ridges of the plaster.

Ways with wallcovers

Paintable textured wallcovering is a chore to remove and may conceal problem plaster. Instead of removing it, make a feature of the texture with color-washing and bagging effects. Or add metallic highlights or spattered color to give textured wallcovering a completely fresh look.

2 Color-wash in green

● Prepare a color-wash in your second chosen color by mixing flat latex paint and water in a ratio of 1 to 5 in a paint pail. Add the water to the paint, mixing well, and then brush over the painted wallcovering.

3 Painting the bag

● Wearing a pair of disposable gloves, scrunch up a black plastic trash bag in one hand. With a medium-sized paintbrush in your other hand, paint a little of the satin-finish latex base color on the crumpled surface of the bag, taking care not to overload it.

4 Bagging on

● Hold the crumpled bag firmly and dab it randomly over the color-washed wallcovering to give a scattered pattern of cream. Reapply paint to the bag as necessary. This creates a third level of color over the wall and breaks up the texture.

1 The base color

● Select a base color in satin-finish latex paint, bearing in mind that it will partially show through the color-washing over the top. Paint over the wallcovering, using a large paintbrush and working the paint into all the pits in the texture of the paper. Let dry 2–4 hours.

IDEAS

BAGGING ON
Unlike bagging off, which is a subtractive technique, bagging on adds color and texture in a similar way to sponging. Depending on the coarseness of your bag (which can be plastic or paper), you can create soft, close speckling or strong, defined lines.

COVER-UPS
If a plaster wall is so badly marked or pitted in places that it is beyond repair, disguise it by hanging a patterned rug, a patchwork quilt or a tapestry over the worst of the damage. Wallhangings can look really striking over rough plaster and also can help to create a warm and cozy atmosphere.

DISTRACTIONS
Brighten up a plain expanse of wall with a display of small framed pictures or decorative plates. This will divert the eye from lingering on an uneven surface.

COLOR-WASHING
Rather than attempt to cover particularly rough walls, take the opposite approach and use a technique such as color-washing to accentuate the texture.

STENCILING
Simple stencils in strong shapes and bold colors are very effective over a textured finish. A stenciled border or a random scattering of decorative motifs are quick and simple ways of breaking up a large area of textured wall.

145

Highlighting wallcoverings

All you need for this dramatic and elegant effect is a plain background of paintable textured wallcovering, a gold oil-based stencil crayon and a small paintbrush. Use this clever technique to highlight an alcove or a chimney.

1 Base color

● For a solid background, especially if you are painting over a light base with a dark color, cover textured wallcovering with two coats of flat latex paint. Let dry 2–4 hours between coats.

2 Gold detailing

● Remove any paper from around the stencil crayon and holding it on its side, gently rub it across the wallcover. As it catches on the contours of the paper, it will leave behind gold flecks. Rub the crayon over the whole area.

Spattering

The quick and easy technique of spattering uses a birch whisk to flick specks of color over a plain painted surface. Add interest to walls by painting a plain color below a chair rail and spattering the area above to give a speckled, broken texture.

1 Paint above rail

● Paint the wall above and below the chair rail with flat latex paint in complementary colors. Always use the brighter or heavier of the two colors below the chair rail.

2 Spattering

● Mask off the chair rail and the wall below it with masking tape and paper. Dilute the flat latex paint in the spattering color with half the quantity of water and mix well. Dip a birch whisk into the mixture and, using a flick of the wrist, spatter the area above the rail. Remove the masking tape and paper.

3 A soft effect

● Using a small paintbrush, gently work in circular strokes over the crayon marks. Because it is soft and oil-based, the metallic effect is easy to soften. Work the gold into the textured surface until it has a soft, burnished look.

Textured paints

Today's supple textured paints can seal minor cracks and camouflage small bumps in a primed plaster wall, and they can also be applied to give distinctive textured patterns. Use one of a choice of texturing tools, then choose a paint technique to complement the finish. This background was textured in circles with a coarse stippling brush and allowed to dry for four to six hours. Next, it was painted light yellow, and then lightly brushed across the ridges with a sponge very lightly dabbed in a darker yellow.

Select your materials from the following:
● Textured paint
● Powdered or ready-mixed repair plaster
● Flat latex paint
● Textured roller
● Texturing comb
● Plastering float
● Coarse texturing brush
● Fine texturing brush
● Paint tray

E Q U I P M E N T

Textured roller

● Pour textured paint into a tray and load a coarse-textured roller. Roll it in different directions over the surface, working slowly to avoid splashing. The more you roll, the finer the texture will be.

Brushed circles

● Apply textured paint to the wall with a brush, working outward in areas of about 3 square feet. Hold a coarse-textured plastic stippling brush flat on the wet surface and make overlapping circles by rotating your wrist.

Brushed swirls

● Apply the textured paint in areas as above. Hold a fine texturing brush flat on the surface and draw it across the paint in a series of continuous overlapping swirls over the brushed area.

Plaster techniques

Today, plastering is not just for builders and do-it-yourself experts. With easy-to-use repair plaster, anyone can patch damage or give a soft, textured finish to a whole wall. Buy it in powder form or ready-mixed, apply it with a float, then texture or pattern it. After four to six hours it is dry and can be primed and painted.

Plastering

● Mix the powder form of plaster with water, according to the maker's instructions. Load an upturned float with plaster and tip it up to the wall, spreading the plaster to give a smooth, even finish. Work in areas of about 3 square feet, washing any hardened plaster off the float and softening the surface with a little water to keep it workable.

Rough-cast plastering

● While the plaster is still wet, rough up the surface by digging into it with the side of the float. Create a random, choppy pattern by changing the direction of your hand as you work across the surface. Create a smoother or coarser pattern by adjusting the tilt of the float.

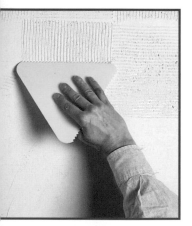

Combed plaster

● Once you have plastered an area of about 3 square feet smoothly, dampen a wide-toothed comb in water and draw it through the plaster in a checkerboard-square pattern. Wipe the comb clean and rinse regularly to keep the teeth clean.

To apply primer or paint over a heavily patterned finish, work the brush firmly into the ridges and troughs to make sure you get complete coverage. Use a flat latex paint for a soft, chalky finish.

Sandstone effect

This is an ideal technique to use on slightly pitted plaster. It only takes a few steps to transform a roughly plastered wall into a clever imitation of sandstone, with its gentle colors and natural aged appearance.

1 Apply the base coat

● If the plaster is untreated, prime it as on page 143. Apply an even covering of white flat latex paint, using a wide paintbrush and working it well into the plaster. If this does not give adequate cover, apply a second coat when the first has dried.

YOU WILL NEED:

- Primer (see page 143)
- White flat latex paint
- Ready-to-use color-wash (we used Paint Magic's buff)
- Artist's acrylic color in burnt umber
- 2½" paintbrush
- 2" paintbrush
- Badger-hair softener
- Fine artist's brush
- Household sponge
- Long metal ruler and pencil
- Craft knife or utility knife
- Masking tape
- Fine-grade sandpaper

2 Apply the color-wash

● Using a household sponge, spread the color-wash thinly over the wall, working outward to cover an area of about 3 square feet at a time and softening the overlap lines with a badger-hair softener as you work. Allow to dry.

3 Marking the lines

● Using a metal ruler and a pencil, draw the outlines of large blocks on the wall: 10" x 20" is a good block size. Align the ruler with each pencil line, and score along the edge of the ruler with a craft knife or a utility knife.

4 Painting the outlines

● Working from the top of the wall, mask off the scored lines ¹/₁₆"–¹/₈" wide, with one strip of tape above the line and another below. Dilute the acrylic color with water, and paint in the lines with a fine artist's brush.

5 Remove the masking tape

● When the painted outlines are dry, gently peel away the masking tape on either side of the scored marks to reveal straight lines.

6 Sanding down

● Finally, to imitate the look of mellowed sandstone, gently rub down the wall with fine-grade sandpaper. This gives a gently distressed look and helps soften hard outlines. Sand the wall in sections of about 3 square feet until the wall is completely covered.

DESIGN ideas

Roughly plastered walls need not limit you to the rustic look—depending on how you treat them, they can look sophisticated, modern or classical.

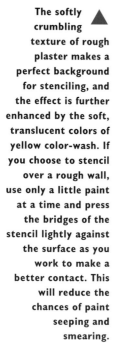

Bright yellow gives this small studio room a warm, Mediterranean atmosphere, and the coarse texture of the walls lends a Bohemian charm to an artist's room. Contrasts of texture, such as that between the painted woven wicker panels and the crusty plaster of the walls, add to the visual interest in the room. ▶

▲ The softly crumbling texture of rough plaster makes a perfect background for stenciling, and the effect is further enhanced by the soft, translucent colors of yellow color-wash. If you choose to stencil over a rough wall, use only a little paint at a time and press the bridges of the stencil lightly against the surface as you work to make a better contact. This will reduce the chances of paint seeping and smearing.

▲ An old-fashioned, high-ceilinged bathroom takes on a look of faded classical elegance with a false sandstone effect over the plasterwork. The block lines have been worked in a lighter color over the buff color-wash of the background to give the impression of aging mortar.

◀ As this painted stone wall shows, there is no need to adhere to rustic or natural colors when treating uneven surfaces. Anything goes—the only caution is to be sure that you work the paint well into all the nooks and crannies so as not to leave unsightly gaps.

CHAPTER 4

Color and Style

The bathroom collection

Discover the fun of stenciling on glass and find out how to transform a plain shower curtain with stenciled motifs. Use these versatile designs to give your bathroom a new look, from the walls right down to the floor.

Bathrooms often need a little warming up, and you can transform a plain bathroom with this collection of versatile designs, using different techniques to work on fabric, glass, tiles and plastic for an allover face-lift.

Take your pick of motifs from the Bathroom Stencil Collection—angelfish, shells, starfish, seahorses and seaweed—to decorate your bathroom with a marine theme. Use fabric paints to stencil on muslin and make a delicate shower curtain or create a frosted design on a glass-fronted cabinet. For a different dimension, add a stenciled design to a plain floor to complete the seashore look. You can use the motifs singly or as a border to suit your bathroom and accessories. Try a few extra decorative touches with glitter and beads for some spectacular results.

EQUIPMENT

YOU WILL NEED:
- The Bathroom Collection stencil, p. 179
- Approximately 3 yds of muslin
- White fabric paint
- Sponge or foam cutouts
- Ruler
- Pen
- White cardboard, approximately 8" x 17"
- Masking tape
- Chalk
- Brown paper

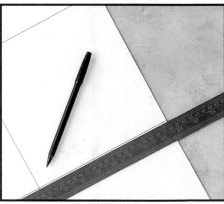

1 Draw the grid

- Mark the cardboard at 8" intervals along each long edge; connect the points to form a grid.

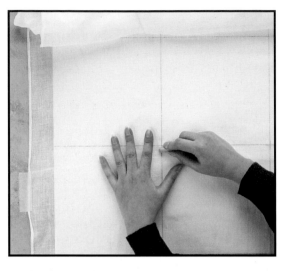

2 Mark the muslin

● On a firm surface, center your grid beneath the lower section of muslin, then tape the muslin taut over it. Transfer the cross points of the grid onto the muslin, using chalk (tailors' chalk is best). Repeat over the rest of the fabric.

3 Prepare the muslin

● Lay out a sheet of brown paper and tape it matte side up to a table so it will absorb any excess stencil paint. Tape the muslin over the top of the brown paper so that it is taut and smooth. (If you don't have a large enough tabletop for the job, work on the floor.)

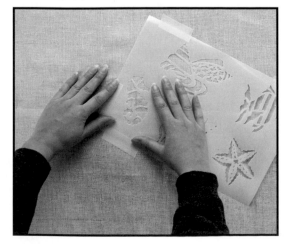

4 Position the first stencil

● Center the first motif over one of the chalk marks and tape it in place with masking tape. (It is best if you de-tack the tape first by dabbing it over a piece of fabric, so that you don't pull the delicate threads of the muslin when you remove it.)

5 Sponge the stencil

● Dip a piece of sponge into the white fabric paint and dab off any excess. Sponge the stencil sparingly, building up the paint cover gradually to avoid bleeding under the stencil bridges.

Stencil a tiled floor

Select your favorite motif from the stencil for use on a bathroom floor covered with painted wood tiles. Make sure the tiles are dry and grease-free before you begin, then tape the stencil to the floor, using masking tape. Choose an oil-based paint and apply it with pieces of sponge or foam cutouts. Use the tiles as a grid to work out a pattern to cover the whole floor. When the paint is completely dry, apply several coats of polyurethane varnish, sanding lightly between the coats.

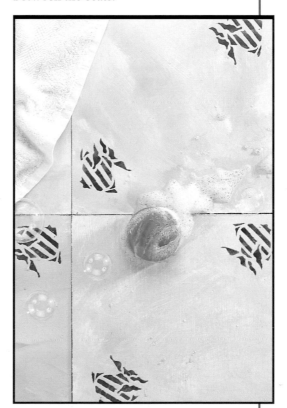

SHOWER CURTAIN

If muslin is not a practical option for your bathroom, or if you just want to brighten up an ordinary plain plastic shower curtain, stencil straight onto the plastic. Try to work on a large, even surface—you don't need a layer of paper underneath.

PLAN YOUR PATTERN

If you abut your curtain grid with the edge of the muslin, your first motif will appear 8" in from the edge, so center the grid beneath the fabric so that the pattern begins 4" closer to the edge.

WHICH PAPER?

If you have any construction paper or wallpaper, don't bother to buy brown paper. As long as the paper is thick and absorbent, anything will do—but do not use newspaper.

USING STENCILS

You may find it easier to work with the stencils cut out individually. The buildup of paint tends to make them sticky, so wipe them clean from time to time.

6 Repeat the pattern

● Working from left to right, stencil the fish, the seahorse and the starfish in a line across the curtain. Continue stenciling, repeating the pattern in staggered rows. You will need to lift the muslin carefully away from the paper every few minutes (or as soon as the paint is dry) to prevent it from sticking to the paper.

7 Finish the curtain

● Hem the base of the curtain so that it matches the length of your shower liner, then machine-stitch it to the top of the liner.

Make a border

Stencil a repeat pattern border in water-based paints. There is no need to stick to aquatic colors—experiment with ochers, reds and greens (below) for a different look, practicing blending colors on scraps.

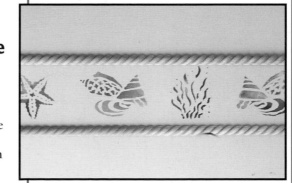

Stenciling on glass

YOU WILL NEED:
- The Bathroom Collection stencil, p. 179
- A little white flat latex paint
- Natural sponge
- Marking pen
- Thin cardboard
- Scissors
- Self-adhesive plastic
- Masking tape

1 Trace the stencil

● Decide which motifs you would like to use on your glass-fronted cabinet or shower door, and trace them from the stencil onto a piece of thin cardboard.

2 Making templates

● Use a marking pen to connect the gaps in the motifs, giving them solid outlines, then cut out.

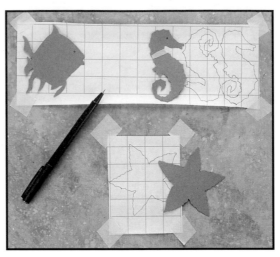

3 Transfer the designs

● Trace around your templates onto the reverse side of the self-adhesive plastic and carefully cut out the shapes, using a pair of sharp scissors.

4 Position the motifs

● Arrange the motifs on the glass door until you are happy with the overall design, then peel off the backing and stick them smoothly into place.

5 Sponging

● Pour a little white paint into a saucer, dilute with just a little water and dab over the glass for a frosted look.

6 Remove the motifs

● Peel away the plastic motifs to reveal the masked-off designs.

Glitter effects

YOU WILL NEED:
- The Bathroom Collection stencil, p. 179
- Metallic stencil paint
- Glitter or glitter glue
- Polyurethane varnish
- Artist's brush
- Masking tape
- Scissors

1 Make glitter varnish

- Mix a little glitter into a quantity of varnish, depending on how bold or subtle you want the finished effect to be.

2 Highlight your stencils

- Using an artist's brush, highlight areas of your stenciled border or other stenciled areas with the glitter varnish. If you prefer, you can do this after the paint has dried but before you remove the stencil.

If you are stenciling a glass or plastic shower door, stencil the outside of the door, as the continuous contact with water from condensation and from the shower spray will wear the paint away.

Metallic stencil paints on dark backgrounds look very effective. If you are using glitter glue, simply dab it onto the stencils to add highlights.

Suns &
MOONS

Give your home a celestial touch with these stylish sun and star motifs. Stenciled in a repeat pattern in gold on a pale base, they give a fresh feel to any room.

Transform a plain wall with the glitter of gold suns and stars. Used to form a repeat pattern, the motifs create the look of expensive hand-printed wallpaper. You do not need to use elaborate measuring techniques—a cardboard template provides a shortcut to symmetrical spacing.

You can use the sun, stars and moon in various combinations: Stencil the entire swag of stars or pick out one star to stencil separately. Enlarge your stencils by photocopying and recutting, and use the motifs as dramatic decoration on furniture.

Planning your pattern

The sun-and-star repeat pattern is based on a diamond-shaped group of motifs, positioned using the template. The template is based on a 4⅜" square, but you can reduce or enlarge its size to alter the spacing of the pattern. Move the elements closer for maximum impact or further apart for a lighter feel.

The silver swags, shown on page 162, are positioned using a plumb line as a guide. The lines are then repeated regularly for a dramatic effect.

YOU WILL NEED:
- Suns and Moons stencil, p. 180
- Metallic stencil paint in gold
- Glitter glue
- Stencil brush
- Fine artist's brush
- Cardboard
- Ruler
- Craft knife
- Plumb line
- Chalk
- Pencil
- Masking tape
- Spray adhesive
- Tape measure
- Cutting mat

1 Position the template

● Cut a 4³⁄₈" square template from the cardboard. Using the plumb line as a guide, position the template diagonally on the wall; the string should fall through the top and bottom corners. Mark the wall at each corner point.

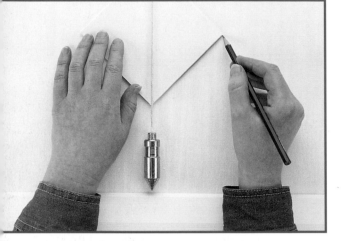

2 Position the stencil

● The pencil marks form a diamond shape. Starting at the left hand dot, position the large star motif. The tip of its right arm should line up with the dot, so that the star sits outside the diamond guide. Tape into place, then stencil, using the gold stencil paint and the stencil brush.

3 Stencil the first pattern

● Stencil a pattern of four motifs, with a star at either side of the diamond pencil marks, and suns at the top and bottom. Take care when positioning each motif that they all sit at the same angle.

4 Mark the second pattern

● Working across the wall from left to right, place the template so that one corner abuts the tip of the right-hand star. Again, use the plumb line as a guide. Mark at the top, right and bottom corners.

5 Stencil second pattern

● Stencil a second diamond pattern alongside your first, but this time with the left-hand arm of the star on the pencil dot.

6 Trim the template

● Stencil the repeat pattern over the entire area, following steps 4 and 5. When you have finished, make a guide for drawing the gold lines between motifs by cutting the template to size. Place squarely on the cutting board and trim down one side, 1" from the edge.

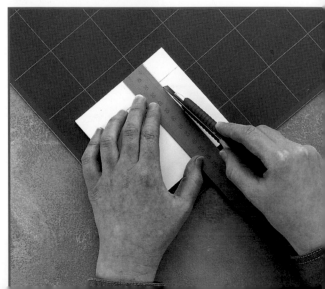

7 Cut to a square

● To make the new template easier to use, trim 1" off the top to cut the template into a square. (This will enable you to use all sides when painting the link lines.)

When you are stenciling the repeat pattern, it is important to position each subsequent motif correctly. You can double check your pencil guides with the tape measure and plumb line.

8 Paint the gold lines

● Hold your cut-to-size template between a sun and star motif. Using the fine artist's brush, paint a gold line along the edge. Repeat over the entire design. Clean the template from time to time, so that the paint does not smudge onto your pattern.

161

Swag room

For a dramatic, luxurious look, stencil swags of silver stars on a vibrant blue background. Add the finishing touch with bold stenciled accessories.

YOU WILL NEED:
- ● Suns and Moons stencil, p. 180
- ● Metallic stencil paint in silver
- ● Stencil brush
- ● Masking tape
- ● Plumb line
- ● Tape measure
- ● Chalk
- ● Spirit level

2 Stencil the right side of the pattern

● Stencil the first swag, using the silver metallic paint and the stencil brush. Work from the top down, so that you do not smudge the paint.

3 Mark the position of large star

● Reposition the stencil. Place the swag so that the large star from the center sits underneath your stenciled motif; tape into place. Using the chalk, mark two small points inside the top and bottom of the star.

4 Stencil other side

● Stencil all the way down the right side of the plumb line. Remember to mark spaces for the large star. For the other side of your swag, make sure the first strand is touch dry, then position the stencil as in step 1, measuring ½" from the left side of the plumb-line string. Complete the strand.

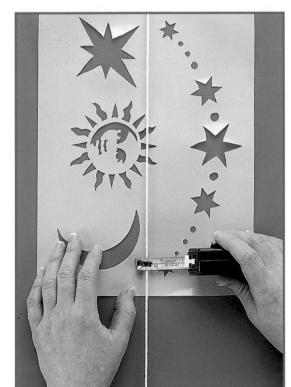

1 Position the stencil

● Starting at the top of the wall, tape the plumb line in position. Then, using the string as a guide, position the swag ½" to the right. Measure at the top and bottom of the motif, to ensure the stencil is straight. Tape into position.

It is important to keep your plumb-line string straight, as it acts as your guide for stenciling all the swags. A piece of resuable adhesive, placed behind the string just above the weight, will fasten it to the wall.

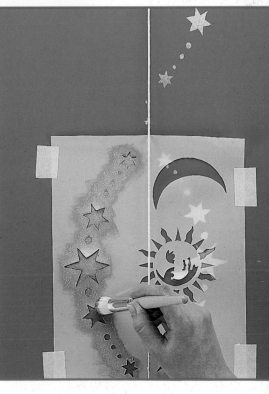

5 Mark position of next strand

● Using the tape measure, spirit level and chalk, mark 10½" from the plumb-line string at the center, top and bottom of the motif. Repeat these measurements for all the swags.

6 Stencil large stars

● Making sure that your stenciled stars are touch dry, reposition the large star motif over the chalk marks made in step 3. Tape into position, taking care not to mask over your motifs. Stencil, using silver paint and the stencil brush. Repeat this process for the entire strand.

7 Work down the second strand

● Move the plumb line so that the string lies on top of the chalk marks in step 5. Then repeat steps 1 through 4, in order to stencil the second column of swags.

Star and moon tray

Brighten a plain tray with this striking sun-and-moon design. Choose two contrasting colors for maximum impact—here, we used yellow and purple. Paint the tray with a base coat of yellow. Using the stencil, draw sun and moon outlines on cardboard and cut out. Using a random pattern, secure the cardboard stars and moons to the tray with spray adhesive. Paint on the top coat, allow to dry, then remove all the cardboard shapes.

Trailing vine

Discover the hidden potential
of stencil motifs to extend
their design, and find out how
to stencil on ceramics.

PHOTOGRAPHY BY LIZZIE ORME

2 Trace the motifs

● Tape the stenciled design to a work surface, using masking tape. Place a piece of stencil acetate over the first motif you want to copy; if necessary, hold the acetate in place with masking tape. Trace the outline of the motif, using a felt-tipped pen. Cut off the piece of acetate, allowing at least 1¼" all around the design. Repeat with other motifs you wish to copy.

YOU WILL NEED

● **Trailing Vine stencil, p. 181**
● **Water-based stencil paints in greens, purple, brown and yellow, plus one dark color**
● **Mixing palette**
● **Pieces of sponge**
● **Masking tape**
● **Scissors**
● **Stencil acetate**
● **Felt-tipped pen**
● **Cutting mat**
● **Craft knife or utility knife**
● **Colored chalk**
● **Plumb line**
● **Tape measure**
● **String**

Designs such as a leafy branch, a stem of flowers or, as shown here, a vine, can be adapted to be much more flexible than just the one motif on its own. Use the separate elements of the stencil to extend its scope.

Although it is possible to mask off individual areas of the stencil, it saves the trouble of masking and remasking if you cut a selection of mini-stencils to use as you need them. Follow these simple steps to cut a selection of leaves, stems and bunches of grapes. You will then have all the elements you need to extend the main stencil and create shaped designs, as well as small motifs for decorating accessories or furniture.

Using stencil pieces

This is an ideal way to adapt a stencil to fit around the features of a room or to work as a tailor-made frame to furniture or fixtures. Since stencils are made up of separate elements, it does not matter if you combine these differently to fit a particular shape or use single pieces as highlights. If you are not completely confident about building up a stenciled shape, practice on a piece of scrap paper until you get the effect you want.

3 Cut stencils

● Secure the acetate with the traced motif to a cutting mat, using masking tape. Cut around the outline of the motif, using a craft knife or a utility knife. For a clean outline, cut from the elbow, rather than the wrist—this gives a more fluid movement in following the shape of the design.

4 Mark the wall

● To fit a stencil design over the top of a shelf, draw a chalk line or a pencil line on the wall at the top of the shelf; remove the shelf. Suspend a plumb line above the line, then measure and mark your chosen distance at right angles from the shelf line. Repeat to give a mark the same distance above the other end of the shelf.

1 Stencil a template

● To make mini-stencils from a large design, first make a template. Attach the stencil to a piece of thick paper with masking tape and stencil in a dark color to create a one-color design. Allow to dry.

5 Mark a line

● Attach a piece of string to one of your marked points, using masking tape or a push pin. Run a piece of chalk along the string as you unroll it to reach the second chalk mark. Secure the string just beyond the second mark so that it covers both marks; using your thumb and forefinger, lift the string away from the wall. Let it twang back to leave a perfect chalk line. Remove the string from the wall.

6 Stenciling

● Place the stencil so that it is level over the middle of the chalk line and the tip of the bunch of grapes just abuts the line; secure with masking tape. Stencil in blended shades of green, purple and brown. Continue on both sides to the extent of the shelf, flopping alternate stencils.

7 Mini-stencils

● Using one of the individual leaf stencils, position it with the stem close to the main stencil at the end of the stenciled strip. The aim is to create a cascade of leaves and grapes that tapers naturally down both sides above the shelf.

8 Building the stencil

● Make sure that the additional motif is dry. Position a bunch of grapes with its stem among the existing leaves so that the fruit trails just below the chalk line. Stencil as before. When this is dry, continue the trail of leaves and stems, sometimes flopping the stencils for variety. Take care in shaping the way the vine hangs down one side of the shelf.

9 Final touches

● Add the last, tapering leaf to the right side of the shelf. For an unusual and eye-catching effect, repeat the trail of leaf and grape stencils on the other side, this time extending it at least 12" below the stenciling on the right.

A loose trail of contrasting leaves gives a coordinated feel to a plain painted chair.

Use separate elements from the vine stencil to accessorize painted furniture in a room where you have stenciled the walls. Just a few leaves can look remarkably effective.

● Elements taken from the Vine stencil, p. 181

YOU WILL NEED

- Ceramic stencil paint in white and shades of green and purple
- Plain ceramic plate
- Small paintbrush
- Pieces of sponge or foam cutouts
- Clean lint-free cloth
- Small bowl
- Spoon for mixing
- Masking tape

Transform a plain plate with ceramic paints. Baked-on colors can be washed without spoiling.

There is no great secret to stenciling on ceramics—you simply need to use specialized paints and follow the manufacturer's instructions carefully to achieve a permanent and washable finish. This usually involves baking the painted item in the oven, so make sure that your chosen piece is fireproof before you start.

Stencil pieces

Follow the steps to cutting ministencils on pages 166–167, then use these to compose a motif on a plate or other piece of crockery. Although it is easy to stencil on surfaces that are curved, it is much harder to bend a stencil to fit closely to a rounded shape, so for best results, avoid stenciling on bowls.

Freehand details

Once you have decorated your plate with a stenciled motif, you might like to add a simple painted border around the flat central area. Although this does not need to be perfectly precise, it is probably best to divide the circumference of the plate into halves, quarters and so on, so that you get fairly even spacing. Once you get a taste for decorating your plain crockery, there is no limit to the effects you can achieve. Try ceramic paints for stenciling, stamping and freehand painting, or experimenting with sponging or ragging to give other background textures to design on.

Whatever planning you need to do over the painted background, do not make any marks in pencil or chalk until the paint has been made permanent by baking. Until it is baked on, ceramic paint will start to lift off in a thin skin.

1 **Prepare the plate**

● Make sure that the plate you want to decorate is completely clean, free of grease and dry. Prepare it by washing the plate thoroughly, then wipe dry with a clean lint-free cloth to avoid getting small fibers stuck in the paint. If you are painting more than one plate, prepare all of them in the same way before starting to paint each one with the background color.

2 **Background color**

● Ceramic paints mix easily, so you can blend a background color to suit your room. Mix enough to cover all the plates, with some left over in case of stenciling corrections. Paint over the plate in even strokes, covering neatly just over the lip. Bake according to the manufacturer's instructions.

3 **Blending colors**

● For stenciling, you may find that the ceramic paints are a little too thick. If so, thin a little at a time by pouring some of the paint into a small bowl and adding water a couple of drops at a time until you reach the right consistency.

4 Planning

● Do not attempt to stencil over the background color until you have planned exactly how the motifs will look on the finished plate. Take the different elements you wish to use and try them in different positions on the flat central area of the plate. The finished design should look balanced and be contained within the center of the plate. Only start arranging your design after baking the background; even light pressure on an unbaked surface can start to lift the paint. Start the design with the central motif, securing it in place with masking tape.

Separating out elements of a large stencil gives you great scope for creating new designs and shapes—and you can expand this even farther if you enlarge or reduce the size of these elements by photocopying and cutting new stencils.

5 Stencil the grapes

● With a little of your chosen colors poured onto a plastic plate or into a palette, pick up a little purple on a piece of sponge; wipe off the excess paint as you would with water-based acrylic paints and dab sparingly over the grapes. Blend the colors as you work, adding shades of blue or mauve for a more realistic appearance. Do not apply too much paint, as smudged edges are hard to rectify. Let dry completely before adding the next piece of the design. Use a hair dryer to speed up the drying process.

6 Add the leaves

● Position one leaf stencil, taking care not to stick tape over the grapes. Fill in with shades of green, then when this is dry, add the final leaf. Bake again for about 40 minutes to make the stenciled motifs permanent.

Use the bunch of grapes with its twisted woody stem, flopping the stencil, to add a rustic decoration to the doors of a painted cupboard. The painted effect of the cupboard is achieved by using a soft purplish color wash, applied with a piece of sponge over a plain coat of gray-blue flat latex paint. Use an olive green color wash, applied in the same way over the moldings, to get a slightly distressed appearance.

The nursery collection

Add the perfect personal touch to a nursery with enchanting stenciled motifs—baby animals, flowers and butterflies—and explore the endless scope of accessorizing, even on glass and fabric, using these charming stencil designs.

YOU WILL NEED:
- Nursery Collection stencil, p. 182
- Flat latex paint in white and yellow
- One 1-oz bottle each water-based stencil paint in red, yellow, blue, green, white and brown
- Medium-sized paintbrush
- Household sponge or stencil brushes
- Narrow paintbrush
- Palette
- Tape measure
- Long ruler, soft pencil
- Spirit level
- Masking tape, scissors
- Barley-twist molding
- Miter box, saw
- Fine-grade sandpaper
- Wood glue

EQUIPMENT

U se this collection of versatile nursery motifs to give a coordinated look to a baby's first room. With designs that work as borders, as single motifs and as built-up patterns, you can add your own personal touch to furniture, fixtures, fabrics and accessories.

Try new surfaces
If you have stenciled only on solid surfaces before, try using these pretty motifs to decorate fabric for curtains, upholstery or soft furnishings. If you have never tried stenciling on glass, see how quick and easy it is to transform a plain glass jar into a special nursery storage jar.

For both glass and fabric, the most important point to remember is not to use too much stencil paint, so build up the cover sparingly until you reach the depth of color you want.

Planning
The motifs lend themselves well to borders and allover patterns, but both need careful planning for space and positioning. Although it is time-consuming, effort spent on planning and marking out your stencil area is never wasted!

Nursery designs

● Create a nursery that will appeal to grown-ups too! A trimmed border of stenciled ducklings makes a charming rail between daffodil yellow sponging and soft turquoise color-washing. The look is prettier than wallpaper and has that special personal touch.

1 Marking the border

● If you are splitting your walls between two techniques, mask a horizontal line between them to mark the top of the border. For plain walls, measure a constant height up from the floor; checking with a spirit level, apply masking tape at the level at which you want the top of your border. Mark points 6"–7" below this for the lower edge of the border.

2 The base line

● Using a long ruler and a soft pencil, connect the marks below the existing masking tape; use a spirit level to make sure that the line is perfectly horizontal. Apply a strip of masking tape below the marked edge with its top abutting the pencil line.

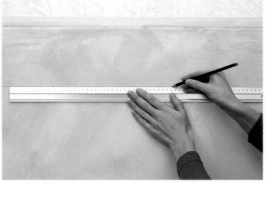

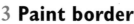

3 Paint border

● Using a medium-sized paintbrush, apply an even coat of white flat latex paint in smooth, horizontal strokes between the two strips of masking tape. As this needs to cover a colored base, allow 2–4 hours to dry completely, then apply a second coat. This should give a solid background for stenciling.

TIPS

■ For a clean finish around the edges of the molding, clean away any glue that has seeped under the edges, using a lint-free cloth dampened with a little water. On external corners, if the join is not perfectly flush, fill the gap with a little all-purpose filler on your finger. When dry, touch up with a little color wash.

4 Ducklings

● Position the duck-and-duckling stencil with the motifs in the center of the border and the top of the stencil parallel with the top masking tape. Stencil the motifs in yellow, orange and blue, with the bullrushes in green, using cut pieces of sponge or stencil brushes. Carefully remove the stencil.

5 Extra ducklings

● Reposition the stencil with the duckling just behind the stenciled one; it does not matter if they are not in a perfect line. Stencil as before, repeating for extra ducklings. Flop the stencil for alternate groups of ducks around the walls.

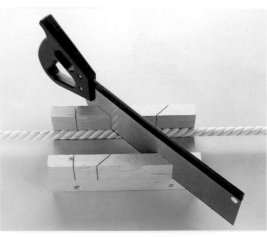

6 Prepare the molding

● Measure the walls and mark lengths on the molding—you will need to cut two pieces for each wall. Place the molding with its back to the side of the miter box and with the end mark at the saw groove. See Help File, opposite, for more details on using a miter box.

174

7 Sanding the molding

● When you have cut the necessary lengths of molding, smooth the ends by sanding lightly with fine-grade sandpaper. The strips should be mitered at the corners of your walls to trim the internal and external right angles all around the room.

8 Color-washing

● Pour a little latex paint in the color you have chosen for the molding into a small paint pail. Pour in an equal quantity of water and stir well. If this is still thick and opaque, add more water until the mixture has the consistency of thin cream.

9 Sponging

● Cut a small piece of sponge, dip it into the color wash and use to color the molding. This sponge method gives a quick and even covering of color and prevents you from using too much color wash on the molding.

10 Applying the glue

● When the color wash on the molding is completely dry—2 hours at most—apply an even coating of wood glue to the back of one piece of molding, using either a very narrow paintbrush or a wide artist's fitch.

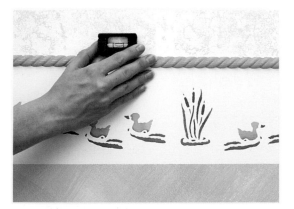

11 Applying the molding

● Place the first glued strip of molding on the wall so that it fits exactly into or around the corner and check that it is perfectly horizontal, using a spirit level. Glue and apply the remaining pieces in turn to complete a double layer of molding all around the room.

MITER BOX
When you cut molding using a miter box, you create two angles: one to fit into a recessed internal corner and one to fit around an external corner. Therefore, when cutting molding for a room with both types of corner, you can alternate the pieces so that you follow one strip with ends cut for an internal angle with a strip cut for an external angle. Remember, when cutting to fit an external corner, that the molding needs to be slightly longer than the wall.

HEAVY MOLDING
If your chosen molding is quite heavy, it may help to hold it in place with masking tape while the glue dries. This will prevent it from slipping out of position. To apply heavier moldings, use the same technique, but reinforce the glue by using nails to keep the border in place.

BORDER PLANNING
The stenciled duck and duckling motifs can be adjusted to fit any width of wall. You can extend the overall size of each group by adding more ducklings or by allowing a little more space between them. On a narrower expanse of wall, you might like to use two flopped motifs with just one duck and duckling. Unlike a wallpaper border, the stenciled motifs can be tailored to fit any width of wall.

Motifs on glass

Stenciling on glass or mirrors can add a perfect finishing touch—and you can use the same water-based stencil paints that you use for stenciling over paintwork or other solid surfaces. The trick is to apply the paint sparingly so that it does not seep under the stencil bridges. Follow these simple steps for crisp and perfect outlines every time.

YOU WILL NEED:
- Nursery Collection stencil, p. 182
- Water-based stencil paints in chosen colors
- Spray varnish
- Pieces of sponge or foam cutouts
- Scissors
- Masking tape or low-tack spray adhesive
- Palette for mixing

1 Positioning the stencil

- To embellish a glass jar, place the motif you wish to stencil on the side of the jar and tape it in place with masking tape. Mask off other areas of the stencil if they are close to the one you want to use. Curved surfaces are easy to stencil on, but for the best results, avoid rounded surfaces.

2 Stenciling

- Pour a little of each of your chosen colors into a palette or saucer and pick up a little of the first color on a piece of sponge. Dab off the excess on scrap paper, then apply the paint thinly so that it will not bleed; you can always restencil the same arca again.

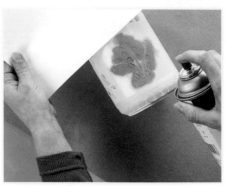

3 Varnishing

- Allow the stenciling to dry completely; then, with the stencil still in place, spray lightly over the motif with spray varnish. This gives spot protective cover against wear and tear without covering the glass jar.

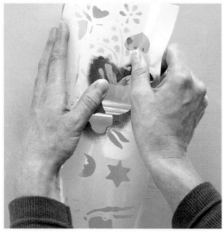

4 Additional motifs

- Remove the stencil; then, when the varnish is dry, reposition the stencil to add different motifs around the existing stencil. Apply stencil paint sparingly, as before, and varnish before lifting the stencil away.

Stencils on fabric

Stenciling on fabric is simple—the important point to remember is that you need to keep the fabric held firmly in position. Some standard water-based paints can be used on fabric (check with the manufacturer's instructions), but it is just as easy to buy special fabric paints for the job.

1 Prepare fabric

- Use a piece of firm cardboard to create a firm base for stenciling. For a small fabric bag, insert cardboard inside the bag.

YOU WILL NEED:
● Nursery Collection stencil, p. 182
● Fabric paints
● Stencil brushes
● Fine artist's brush
● Firm cardboard
● Masking tape
● Scissors
● Palette or saucers
● Scrap paper

3 Mask the stencil

● Stray dabs of paint are hard to remove from fabric, so it is a good idea to mask off any areas of the stencil that you do not want to use. Secure the masked stencil in place with more masking tape on the taut fabric.

4 Stencil in the first color

● Fabric paints are specially formulated so that they will not sink into the fibers of fabric or run but instead they will dry on the surface. Even so, it is advisable to dab the paint on thinly, building up the strength of color gradually.

5 The second color

● On a motif such as the rabbit, add stenciled details in a second color. Load a clean brush with white fabric paint, dab off the excess on scrap paper and apply sparingly on the tail and ears. It does not matter if the two colors merge or overlap—this will add to the charm of the design.

6 Final touches

● Remove the stencil; then, when the stenciled fabric paint is completely dry, use a little white fabric paint on a fine artist's brush to fill in details, such as the eye and, if you want, the nose.

2 Tape down fabric

● Make sure the fabric is completely flat, then tape it down to a firm, flat surface. Make sure the fabric is taut between the strips of masking tape, so that it forms a firm base for stenciling.

TIPS

■ If you find that stencil paint has seeped under the bridges when you are stenciling over glass, wait until the paint is completely dry, then scrape away the excess paint, using a craft knife. Acrylic water-based paints will scrape away easily without scratching the surface of the glass.

■ When stenciling on a mirror or on glass, always make sure that the surface is dry and completely free of grease, so that the paint will adhere.

Stencil Patterns

To cut stencils from the designs on the following pages, use one of the following methods:

- Trace the stencil motif you want to use onto tracing paper, or using a photocopier, enlarge or reduce the motif to the desired size. Tape a piece of stencil acetate over the motif and trace the outline, using a fine-tip permanent marker. Place the acetate on a cutting mat and use a craft knife to cut out the design.

- Photocopy or trace the image, place it on a cutting board and place a sheet of glass on top of the image. Secure a piece of stencil acetate on top of the glass with masking tape and use a heated stencil cutting pen to cut out the design, taking care to follow the manufacturer's safety instructions.

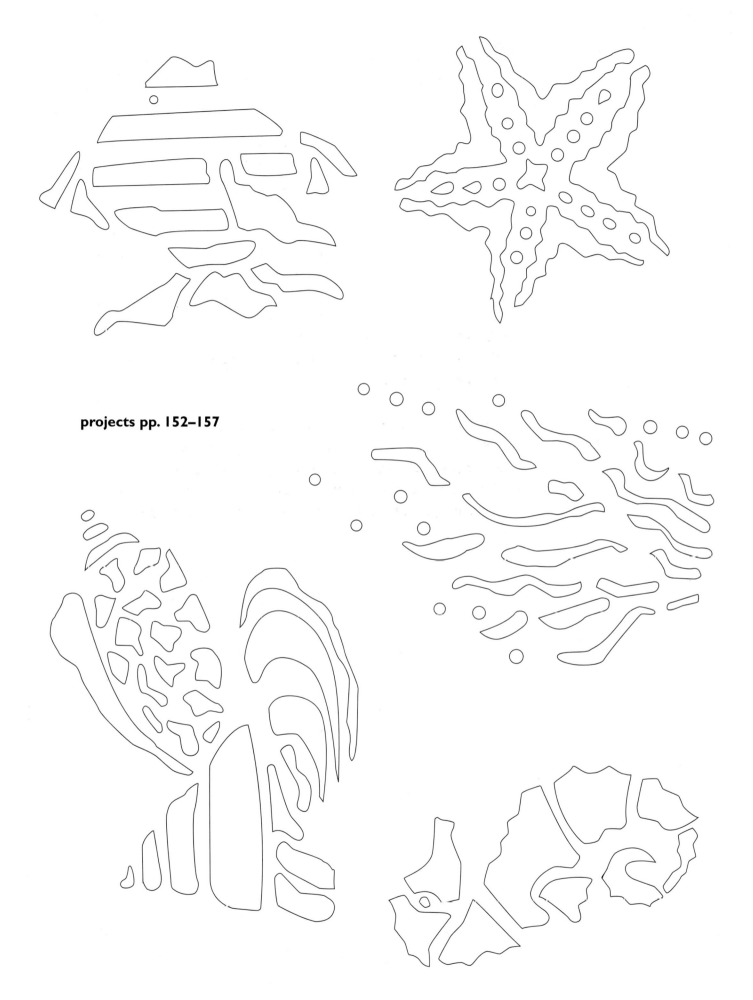

projects pp. 152–157

projects pp. 158–164

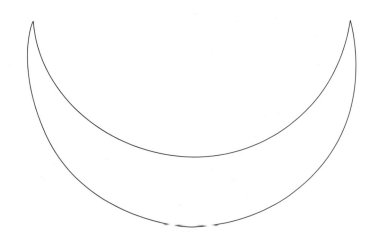

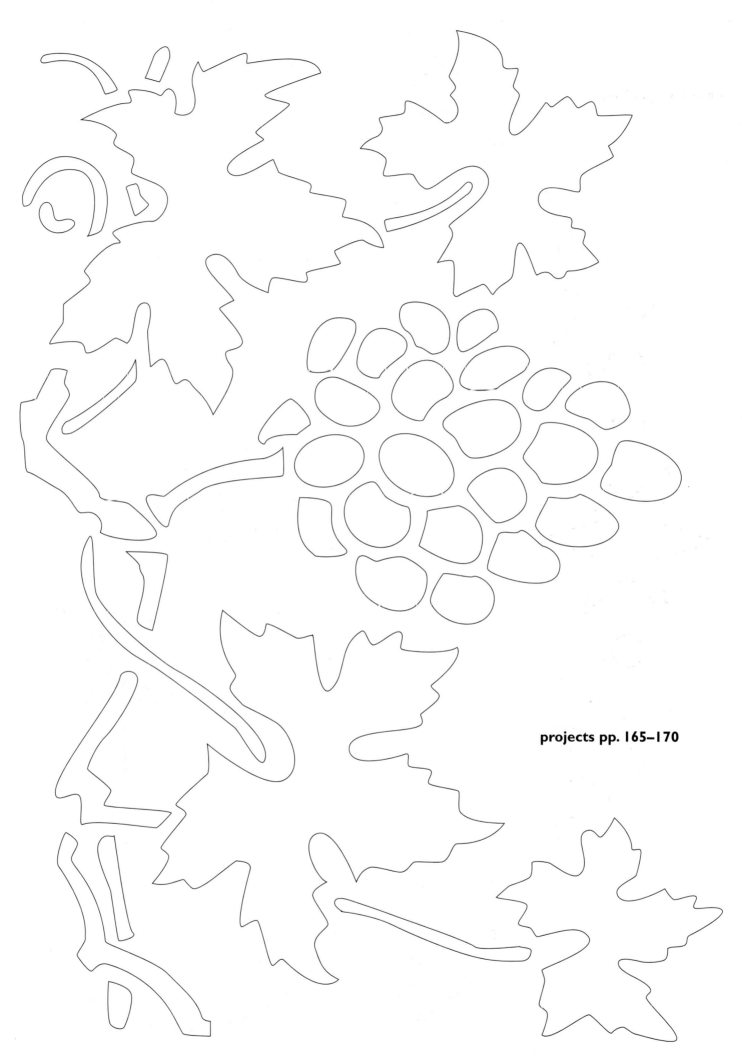

projects pp. 165–170

projects pp. 175–177

BUYER'S GUIDE

Painting supplies and stenciling supplies are readily available at crafts shops, art supply stores and paint stores. Interior latex and oil-based paints and general painting supplies are carried by paint stores, home-improvement centers and hardware stores. Listed below is a sampling of mail-order sources that carry harder-to-find supplies and manufacturers to call for information.

Adele Bishop
3430 South Service Road
Burlington, Ontario, Canada
L7N3T9
800-510-0245
Catalog $4.00, refundable with first order.
Stencil paints, stencil supplies and stencil kits.

Benjamin Moore
51 Chestnut Ridge Road
Montvale, NJ 07645
888-236-6667. Call for nearest local retailer.
Interior and exterior paints, stains and varnishes.

Binney & Smith, Inc.
1100 Church Lane
P. O. Box 431
Easton, PA 18044-0431
800-272-9652. Call for nearest local retailer.
Artist's oil paints, and acrylic paints.

Delta Technical Coatings, Inc.
2550 Pellissier Place
Whittier, CA 90601
800-423-4135. Call for nearest local retailer.
Paint supplies, including stencil paint, acrylic paint, crackle medium, stains, finishes and glazing liquids.

Dick Blick
P. O. Box 1267
Galesburg, IL 61402-1267
800-447-8192
Catalog $5.00, refundable with first order.
Art supplies, including powder pigments, brushes, crackle medium, varnishes, fabric crayons, acrylic paints, acrylic mediums, artist's oil colors, adhesives, faux finishing kits and patina kits.

Duncan Enterprises
5673 E. Shields Avenue
Fresno, CA 93727
209-291-4444. Call for nearest local retailer.
Aleene's acrylic paints and mediums.

Janovic/Plaza
30-35 Thomson Avenue
Long Island City, NY 11101
800-772-4381
Catalog $4.95.
Specialty decorating supplies, including paints, graining combs, graining rollers, varnishes, sealers, glazing liquids and specialty brushes.

Modern Options
2325 Third Street #339
San Francisco, CA 94107
415-252-5580. Call for nearest local retailer.
Free catalog.
Patina Antiquing Kit for verdigris finishing and faux patina supplies.

McCloskey Varnish Company
1191 South Wheeling Road
Wheeling, IL 60090
800-345-4530. Call for nearest local retailer.
Glazing liquids and wood stains.

Paint Effects
2426 Fillmore Street
San Francisco, CA 94115
415-292-7780
Web page: www.painteffects.com
Formerly known as Paint Magic.
Call or use web page to order.
Decorative painting and faux-finishing supplies, including pre-mixed glazes, crackle glazes and color-washing supplies.

Pearl Paint
308 Canal Street
New York, NY 10013-2572
Attn: Catalog Dept.
800-221-6845
Catalog $1.00.
Fine art, craft and graphic discount supplies, including artist's oil colors, powder pigments, acrylic paints, faux finish glazes, mediums, brushes and adhesives

Plaid Enterprises, Inc.
1649 International Ct.
P. O. 7600
Norcross, GA 30091-7600
800-842-4197. Call for nearest local retailer.
Stencil supplies, acrylic paints, brushes, crackle medium, antiquing paint, glazes and graining combs.

Pottery Barn
P. O. Box 7044
San Francisco, CA 94120-7044
800-922-5507. Call for nearest local Decorator Store.
Paint Magic kits for faux finishes are available at Pottery Barn Decorator Stores around the country.

Sax Arts & Crafts
P. O. Box 510710
New Berlin, WI 53151-0710
800-558-6696
Catalog $5.00, refunded with first order; minimum order of $10.00.
Arts and crafts supplies, including artist's oil colors, artist's acrylic colors, powder pigments, stencil paint crayons, fabric crayons, brushes, mediums and palettes.

S&S Worldwide
P. O. Box 513
Colchester, CT 06415-0513
800-243-9232
Free catalog; minimum order of $25.00.
General arts and crafts supplies.

Sherwin-Williams Co.
101 Prospect Avenue
Cleveland, OH 44115-1075
800-474-3794. Call for nearest local retailer.
Complete line of interior and exterior paints and stains.

Thompson & Formby, Inc.
825 Crossover Lane
Memphis, TN 38117
800-367-6297. Call for nearest local retailer.
Wood stains, glazes and faux finishing kits.

INDEX